CW00537198

Christian Dance

for those who can't...

but are willing to give it a try!

Carol Hathorne

MONARCH
BOOKS

Copyright © Carol Hathorne 1999

The right of Carol Hathorne to be identified
as author of this work has been asserted by her in
accordance with the Copyright, Designs
and Patents Act 1988

First published by Monarch Books in 1999

ISBN 1 85424 440 X

All rights reserved.
No part of this publication may be reproduced or
transmitted in any form or by any means, electronic
or mechanical, including photocopy, recording or any
information storage and retrieval system, without
permission in writing from Monarch Books
in association with Angus Hudson Ltd,
Concorde House, Grenville Place,
Mill Hill, London NW7 3SA.

Unless otherwise stated, Scripture quotations are
taken from *The Holy Bible, New International Version*, copyright
© 1973, 1978, 1984 by International Bible Society.
Used by permission of Hodder and Stoughton Ltd.

British Library Cataloguing Data
A catalogue record for this book is available
from the British Library.

Designed and produced for the publishers by
Gazelle Creative Productions,
Concorde House, Grenville Place,
Mill Hill, London NW7 3SA.

Contents

DEDICATION

To Nancy, who got me dancing round the kitchen.

ACKNOWLEDGEMENTS

I acknowledge with grateful thanks all the resources, help and especially inspiration that I have received from the following: Shirley Collins, Paula Douthett, Damien Grantley, Mavis Smith, Julia Myles, Andy Raine, the Wilkinson family, Val Whiley, Kathryn Slater, and all the members of 'Body and Soul', Linda Wells, the Rev. Hannah Lewis, Marie and Andrew Bensley, Gemma Lathe, the late Bob Marsh, the family of the late Fiona Bennett, Andy Au, Angela Courtney, Jan Dyer, Jane Grimshaw, Annie Stones, Kate Jennings, Rowena Webb and Liz and Jean from the Thursday Ladies' dance group.

Introduction

When I was four years old, my grandparents took me away for a week to Butlins holiday camp, Skegness. There I apparently amazed them, and rather disgraced myself, by getting up and dancing, all on my own, right round the ballroom. It was, I should explain, 1948, when children were still supposed to be seen and not heard.

As I grew older, I engaged in dressing up and singing and dancing games, practising steps which my older cousin Evelyn confidently told me were 'tap' on the lino by our front door. But I never had lessons. For me, such things only existed in books like Noel Streatfield's *Ballet Shoes*. And so it was wonderful when rock and roll came along, and I discovered jive, or 'bop' as we called it.

'Bop' was much more important than school, even with those GCEs looming on the horizon. It involved buying flat, black pumps, which were light and flexible to move in, and skirts with layers of net petticoats underneath that flared out gracefully as you moved, running light circles round your partner.

In order to 'bop', you would walk to a crowded dance hall several miles away, and emerge at ten o'clock to catch the bus home with your hair plastered to your head with perspiration and your heart still thumping to the beat of the music.

There was such release in that dancing — it was a healing for teenage woes. No matter what our problems or differences, we were all one in the infectious sway of the jive. That the older generation didn't really approve added to the appeal. Later, when the jive was replaced by other dances, it would still continue to draw. I would long for the moment at family weddings when the music would play and people begin to drift onto the floor, and reality was suspended for the rest of the blissful evening.

Dance and Christianity were never connected in my mind, however, until I went to theological college, although it had been the movements (and the relaxation) of yoga which had drawn me into a sense of the transcendent which was to transform my life, leading me, ultimately, into relationship with Christ.

The West Midlands Ministerial Training Course, based at Queen's College, Birmingham, was ecumenical, training Anglican, Methodist and URC pastors for the ordained ministry. Non-residential and wide ranging, it attracted all kinds of ordinands — many teachers and nurses, but also a photographer, a writer and an actress. And several people who were interested in dance.

There were times when I found the academic side tedious, losing patience with theologians who took ten pages to say what could most effectively be said in one. As an ex-journalist, trained not to waste words, I felt that this was not the way to reach people with the simple good news of the gospel. Apart from that, my image of Jesus Christ was of someone who moved, who prayed, above all, who *lived*, as these dusty books never could.

I darted about at college, making friends, talking, laughing, essentially sharing lives and experiences and vocation with others. And my joy was limitless when I found there were opportunities not only to sing out my love for God, but to dance it too.

At special end-of-term services, and at workshops which were (delightfully!) an option at clergy training days, I threw myself in, literally, with both feet. I hung around, slightly embarrassed, with those rarities the 'real' dancers, the actress ordinand, and the graceful blonde lady who led us in the dance workshop (who I've since learnt was Shirley Collins, who has supplied many of the resources for this book). Still 'dancing on the lino', I secretly hoped some crumb of skill or expertise would somehow miraculously rub off on me.

When my own parish priest led a workshop on relaxation

and movement in worship, I was the first to sign up, lying on the carpet before the dimly lit altar where I had so often knelt to receive the Lord in the holy sacrament. In the midst of a busy life, I was almost painfully eager to listen to the sound of my own breathing, and equate it, in joy and wonder, with that union with the divine I had first sensed in my pre-Christian flirtation with yoga and transcendental meditation.

This, surely, was where God was most simply and power-fully in my life, the heartfelt rhythm of knowledge and accep-tance that truly was 'closer than hands and feet'. What could be more natural than prostrating myself before him in whom I knew I 'lived and moved and had my being'? And if I felt this way, then so, surely, must other Christians — people who perhaps could not, or would not, put their longings into words.

Christian dance does not, on the whole, have a good image in liberal church circles, conjuring up images of mid-dle-aged ladies in flowing robes performing a limited, upper torso display to the accompaniment of rather saccharine music with indistinct words. In my experience, many clergy find it at best mildly amusing, and at worst, embarrassing. In a world where modern ministers tend to be overworked, com-puter bound and professional, it smacks of amateurism and self-indulgence. As a senior bishop once said to me, plain-tively, 'When someone gets up to do liturgical dance, I never know what I'm supposed to *do*!'

In June 1991, I knew exactly what I was supposed to do. Newly ordained to the diaconate, I moved to my first parish, in Wednesbury, West Midlands, with my teenage daughter. The first woman curate at St Paul's and St Luke's, I soon found myself in a routine which came as a gigantic shock to the system.

When the incumbent (a dedicated but very serious-minded priest) had told me at my interview, 'You'll be expected to do sixty hours a week,' and, 'You can forget all that stuff you've been taught at college about taking one session off each day!' I'd thought he was joking.

But weeks into my ministry, I was already experiencing mind-boggling fatigue — mainly from the rapid changes of gear that are all part of parish work. Before my first funeral, I sat down at my vicar's side and told him candidly that I had two fears. One was that I'd press the 'button' and dispatch the body to the waiting oven too soon, and the other was that I'd burst into tears. His expression told me he was not only rather embarrassed, he was taken aback by my openness. I withdrew from the conversation feeling, not for the first time, that my purely instinctive and intensely physical response to things clerical was not quite 'the done thing'.

As the months passed, I blundered through Christmas and Easter, through post-ordination sessions with other just as weary curates. The compulsory deanery chapter meetings gave little joy because ours was a traditionally Anglo Catholic area, where, following the vote on women's ordination to the priesthood, several members subsequently went over to Rome, and others to the anti-female breakaway group 'Forward in Faith'.

'Now just remember,' my vicar said, as he drove me to a chapter meeting I certainly didn't want to attend. 'At one time or another, each of them must have had a vision of Jesus!'

If they had, I never heard them mention it. Instead they talked of shares and systems, reports and recommendations, concepts and commissions. As we all sat, trying to look alert and intelligent, all I wanted was not to sit any more but to get up and move.

My vicar took my training seriously enough to want to help me develop my gifts, even though they were so very different from his own. When I confessed at a staff meeting that, after praying about it, I felt the Lord was calling me to start a Christian dance group, he gave it his whole-hearted support. And that's how 'Exercise in Prayer' was born.

PART ONE

1

Getting Started

For me, 'getting started' meant forming a group called 'Exercise in Prayer' simply because that name had been going round in my head for several years, and I found the play on words irresistible. But whether you begin with a name or not, the launching of a Christian dance group has its problems, and needs lots of thought and even more prayer.

You might find it useful to work through those six 'friends' of Rudyard Kipling that have cut many provincial journalists' teeth: Who? What? When? Where? How? Why?

Who?

Depending on your church situation, the 'Who?' of your dance group should emerge through very necessary advertising on notice-boards, newsletters and parish magazines, as well as by word of mouth.

Be wary of all-inclusive tags like 'all ages welcome' if you intend to encourage people to, for instance, get down on the floor. It sounds obvious, but most elderly people are used to sitting, and can be quite alarmed to enter a room and find it cleared of chairs. Unless they are into keep-fit or aerobics, most over-sixties also equate 'dance' with ballroom, sequence, or at best, rock and roll. So your definition might come as quite a shock to the system! Similarly, young people need to be treated with care, as what might seem not only relevant but trendy to adult Christians is very often hopelessly out of date or 'naff' to teenagers used to dancing along with their current pop icon!

Another familiar tag is 'both sexes', and this is one of which I heartily approve. On the whole, men are notoriously reluctant to take part in dance worship, but interest is growing, and there are several male leaders in the Christian Dance Fellowship of Britain who are beacons in this particular field. Their presence adds a much needed power and energy to dance worship, so if you're lucky enough to get some men interested in joining your group, encourage them all you can.

'Who?' also embraces things like training, experience and expertise. Is the group going to be for absolute beginners, or do you want people who have danced before?

In my situation in Wednesbury, I was grateful to find 'Exercise in Prayer' encouraging one or two of the latter. They became invaluable, suggesting a particular movement, bringing along a piece of music, and generally encouraging the raw beginners to loosen up and let go a little. These were not, I hasten to add, trained dancers, just people who had perhaps taken part in circle dancing at school or college, or, as in one case, someone whose ex-boyfriend had been a member of a liturgical dance group.

The main point about the 'Who?' question is that, with dance, you simply don't have to preach to the converted. Those who have that indefinable 'itch' to do it will come, even if it's only out of curiosity.

As with everything, you do need to pray about it, and also be aware that even when a group has started, its dynamic may be always changing. God has his own reasons for this, so try to be patient and look for his will in the mix of those who come along. Seeing how dance worship can enhance their lives, adding a new dimension and bringing them closer to God and to each other is a wonderful privilege as the weeks and months go by.

What?

The answer to this question depends chiefly on the membership and make-up of your group. Hopefully, the 'What?' will develop and change as the Lord begins to give you new challenges tailor made to your own situation.

If the group is totally inexperienced in dance, it is always best to start with the safe option of calling what you do 'mime', 'movement in worship', or even simply 'praise'. Such a group might well attract the upper-age group, and also not be too threatening to would-be participants who happen to be men.

In my experience, with a beginners' group it is best to concentrate on complete relaxation, seated or lying, followed by prayerful meditation to music which leads into gentle, yoga-type stretches, followed by simple dances before gradually 'winding down' again. The total time should be about one hour.

Excitingly, it was through one of the more able members of my own first group 'Exercise in Prayer' that another Christian dance group came into existence. This was 'Body and Soul', and it marked a transition in my own personal life and ministry, and also became the vehicle for many people to be enabled and released through the spirit of dance so that healing could come, in many guises.

Under the heading of 'What?' this more advanced type of Christian dance group operates through fellowship and sharing. It needs people who are not afraid to talk about the faith that makes them want to dance in worship. People arrive early and never seem to want to go home when the session is over.

Although it is impossible to generalise, this kind of group is more likely to dance in front of other people in church or elsewhere. With encouragement, members will bring dances they have discovered in their own private worship time. They are looking for direction, but happy to participate — spend time in prayer and Bible study as part of the session — and to be aware of God's answers and to rejoice in them (by dancing, of course!).

At the end of this book you will find an example of a relaxation technique, 'warm-up', exercises, meditations, and complete dances which should provide something for everyone, regardless of their experience, expertise and fellowship needs.

When?

When your Christian dance group meets is again a matter of preference. Weekly is good because it safeguards the continuity and relevance of the group, but some groups find it more realistic to meet fortnightly, monthly or even bi-monthly, when it might be possible to have a celebratory Saturday afternoon event, incorporating workshops. Others work best by getting together only when they are actually practising for a special service, so your group might meet in the weeks leading up to Christmas or Pentecost, concentrating on the big event which brings everyone together.

What happened with 'Exercise in Prayer' was, encouragingly, the eventual development of a regular children's dance worship group, while 'Body and Soul' has mushroomed into two separate groups, one for adults and the other comprising the Sunday school of the local Methodist Church.

Meeting outside the regular session with other groups with the same interest also boosts morale and keeps ideas circulating. The Christian Dance Fellowship of Britain holds regular conferences and workshops, including regional days in most areas. These are advertised in their magazine *Tent of David*, as well as in the popular Christian press. Follow up the leads you get and see if the Lord is calling you (or your entire group!) to go along.

Where?

Where your Christian dance groups meets can be a problem unless you have a 'dance-friendly' vicar or minister, so the first thing I advise you to do is check him or her out! Some theological colleges and courses do leave space for dance (as did my own), giving an opportunity for ordinands to try their feet. And clergy conferences, to which the ordained go every couple of years, do sometimes offer this option in worship workshops. So don't assume your vicar will automatically look askance if you ask for the use of the church hall or some other available space. If it is the church hall, it is usually best to offer to pay, even if only a nominal sum, putting things on a proper footing when it comes to heating, lighting, and wear and tear. Your dancers won't mind paying a pound or two, and the arrangement will be much more businesslike.

Church (as opposed to hall) is good. To put it crudely, you already have all the trappings (and the holy atmosphere) and people find it easier to pray in that setting. But churches are notoriously cold buildings, especially on winter evenings, and pews can be a nuisance when you come to perform.

There are alternative places to practise. A friend of mine converted her garage into a proper dance studio with bright yellow curtains, a carpeted floor and a mobile, man-sized cross made to the dimensions in the diagram, kindly donated by dance leader Paula Douthett, which you will find in the back of the book. Weekly dance classes are now held there.

If all else fails, and there are only a few of you, you can dance in the garden. You can practise simple dances in a normal-sized living room or bedroom, so long as you push the furniture back. (Didn't our grandparents used to 'roll up the carpet' to do just that?) If you're organised enough, you can even explore the possibility of hiring school rooms, community centre halls, and private rooms in pubs. The possibilities are endless once you begin to think (and pray) about it.

How?

'How?' is a question which seems to hit us even before we start. How do we dance, particularly if we have been sedentary for nearly half a century and have 'two left feet'? How do we encourage others to join us in praising the Lord in this very upfront way?

Some people find it easy to express themselves in movement. They are supple and tactile, like the girl in my junior school who used to do the splits in the playground and be carried round, shoulder high, by half a dozen other kids. (How I longed to be her!) These are bodily communicators who would, as the old joke goes, be 'speechless if you cut off their hands'. They are also, I suspect, the ones seen raising their hands at church meetings, or unselfconsciously genuflecting or crossing themselves, if that happens to be their tradition.

Others feel clumsy, and the bodily equivalent of 'tongue tied'. They might want to move, but it seems impossible. They don't want to be conspicuous. The bad news is, you have to be conspicuous if you are getting up to dance in church. Unless you are always going to move in worship in the privacy of your room (not that there's an ything wrong with that!), people are going to watch because that's what dance is — an invitation to look and see and hopefully feel all you are trying to express without words.

The planning of your dance group agenda will vary according to what you feel God wants you to achieve, but there are many resources to help you. It's not only advisable, it's essential to plan ahead, so that eventually you build up a repertoire of dances you can produce quite quickly to share with others.

Why?

Arguably the most important question. Why should Christian dance suddenly become part of your life, your worship and your church? Haven't you been perfectly happy without it?

Perhaps the mere fact that you're reading this book is an answer in itself. But if you need convincing further, I'd say movement in worship is definitely good for us — physically, emotionally and spiritually. My own experience is that it is also good for the church — locally, nationally and internationally. Because it does not rely on doctrine, denomination or spoken language, dance can definitely transmit the gospel and 'reach the parts that other worship doesn't'.

At the opening ceremony of the Lambeth conference in July 1998, there was a spectacle of white dresses and clicking heels, and the *Church Times* that week reported that it was the dancers everyone was talking about. Three weeks later, at the closing ceremony, the same newspaper reported that a nun had got up and joyfully danced through the congregation. The conference had not been over, in fact, until the thin nun danced!

Closer to home, I can report that a week-long 'open door' for 600 primary school children held in my parish church recently was totally transformed by the addition of a group of small, ribbon-carrying girls, skipping in the chancel to the singing of 'Jubilate!'.

'Miss! Miss' they demanded, as the act of worship finally came to an end. 'Can't we do it again?'

When something is God's will and purpose, there is always organic growth, and unquenchable interest and enthusiasm, and for this reason alone, many exponents believe God is calling his people to express their love for him and the world he has given us, through the medium of dance. Like many of his bountiful gifts, it also happens to be fun!

2

Dance in the Bible

As my involvement with Christian dance grew, I decided to study certain passages of Scripture where dance is mentioned and where, more specifically, the therapeutic aspects of dance had not been explored.

Dance is actually mentioned twenty-four times in the Bible, nineteen in the Old Testament and five in the New. (For a complete list of these, see Appendix.)

The Old Testament

The Psalms

In the Psalms, we read of the singers and dancers who celebrated Zion, the city of God (Psalm 150:4), and who confessed that place to be the source of light and refreshment: 'All my fountains are in you' (Psalm 87:7). In Psalm 30, the writer changed from his mourning rites to dancing and festal clothing: 'You turned my wailing into dancing' (v 11). All this shows a sense of joy and release expressed in worship of a God who comes with healing in his wings.

Exodus 15

I am personally inspired by the passage in Exodus, which includes the song of Moses and Miriam, which describes graphically how the mighty Lord has hurled the horse and its rider into the sea (Exodus 15:16).

By the obedient movement of the waves which revealed the dry land to the Israelites, the Lord has set free his people, and opened a new path for them, a path that will lead them

19

out of slavery in Egypt to the land flowing with milk and honey. This is expressed in the joyful dance that the prophetess Miriam leads with tambourines, exhorting, 'Sing to the Lord, for he is highly exalted. The horse and its rider he has hurled into the sea' (v 21).

At the breath of the Lord, 'the blast of [his] nostrils' (v 8), we are told the waters piled up — surely an image of God's breath causing the sea to dance back into walls impenetrable except to God's chosen people? 'You stretched out your right hand' (v 12) speaks of a dancing, stretching God, elastic in his reach, majestically awesome in his cleansing power.

Miriam and the women followed the breath of God as they led the celebratory dance of the Israelites into a new, already blessed life, that place of renewal called their promised land.

Judges 11:29–40

This tells the story of Jephthah the Gilead, a mighty warrior who, in exchange for victory over his enemies, made a solemn and terrible vow to the Lord: 'If you give the Ammonites into my hands, whatever comes out of the door of my house to meet me when I return in triumph... will be the Lord's, and I will sacrifice it as a burnt offering' (v 30b).

And who should come out to meet him on his triumphal return to his home in Mizpah, but his only daughter, dancing to the sound of tambourines!

It was customary for women to greet armies returning from battle victoriously in this fashion, and we can perhaps imagine the girl's practice and preparation, the way her heart would leap when she was told her father's entourage was in sight, and it was time for her special performance.

Jephthah must have been in agony when he realised the implication of her joyful dance of welcome and congratulation, and we are told that he tore his clothes, and cried: 'O my daughter! You have made me miserable and wretched, because I have made a vow to the Lord that I cannot break' (v 35).

The un-named daughter knows the strength of the vow —

how the Lord has already fulfilled *his* side of it by avenging her father of his enemies, the Ammonites. She bravely urges her father to do to her just what he has promised, but first begs one request, that she be allowed to 'roam the hills and weep with her friends, because [she] will never marry' (v 37).

Did she, I wonder, also dance with her friends, expressing the bitter regret of her impending death with her body as well, or perhaps instead of, her words? The roaming itself is definitely all about movement, and its poignancy suggests to me a solo dance with all the pathos of the 'dying swan'.

Judges 21:20–25

Dance has always been an integral part of Jewish life. Dance heralds new beginnings, celebrates victories, encourages God's people to look to the future with hope and energy. It undergirds family life, drawing generations together in bonds too deep for mere words.

This passage from Judges describes the annual feast at Shiloh which might have been the Feast of Tabernacles — a harvest festival and also a traditional courtship ritual. It is all about the rebuilding of community after a terrible war which effectively destroyed one of the tribes of Israel, the Benjaminites.

The desperate Benjaminite men hide in the vineyards and then seize wives from among the dancing Shiloh girls whose guardians, brothers or fathers, are negotiated with later. 'While the girls were dancing, each man caught one and carried her off to be his wife. Then they returned to their inheritance and rebuilt the towns and settled in them' (v 23). This life-changing dance can also be said to be a celebration of the Lord's work in creation, and of human sexuality, for according to Martin Bloggs (quoting the *Encyclopedia Judaica*): 'The story of the capture of brides by the surviving Benjaminites indicates that choosing brides during vineyard dances was a recognised practice of Israel.*

---

* Martin Bloggs, *Dance and the Christian Faith* (Hodder and Stoughton, London, 1985), p 26.

The New Testament

In the New Testament there are fewer direct references to dance. Its importance in Jewish family and community life was still paramount, however, as demonstrated by Jesus himself.

In comparing the Jews to sullen, unresponsive children, he says, 'We played the flute for you, and you did not dance' (Matthew 11:17), thus indicating that a refusal to participate in the natural, joyful activity of dancing meant a hardness of heart that denied a potentially close and therefore healing relationship.

In complete contrast to this, Jesus' ministry was one of movement, and most particularly, of touch. He took people by the hand in order to heal them, whether they were an elderly lady like Peter's mother-in-law, or a little girl like Jairus' daughter. He used his own saliva to make salve for a blind man's eyes, and was not afraid to be tactile when ordering the stoppage out of a dead man's ears.

In turn, others responded spontaneously and physically, touching the hem of his garment, wiping his feet with hair and sweet-smelling ointment, ultimately even betraying him with the deadly choreography of a kiss.

Luke 15:11–32

The well-loved parable of the prodigal son shows dance in its usual celebratory role. The best robe has been laid out, the ring and sandals placed on the person of the beloved younger son, the fatted calf duly sacrificed. It is indeed time to have a party, and what good is a party without dancing?

We are not told what form this dancing took, but it was certainly a very outward and visible sign of the restored relationship between the prodigal and his father, a father who, contrary to the conventions of that time and culture, actually ran to meet his errant son, threw his arms around him and kissed him.

This, the expression of the unconditional love that is often compared to the love of God, might well have resulted in both father and son participating in a dance. Anticipating such a dance — the traditional Hebrew celebration of men greeting men — no wonder the dependable elder brother felt spurned and disgruntled.

'I… never disobeyed your orders. Yet you never gave me even a young goat so I could celebrate with my friends. But when this son of yours who has squandered your property with prostitutes comes home, you kill the fattened calf for him!' (vs 29–30).

Acts 3:1–10

The crippled man at the Temple gate called Beautiful asked Peter and John for money, but received something much more precious and life changing. Ordering him in the name of Jesus Christ of Nazareth to get up and walk, Peter took him by the right hand and helped him to his feet. Immediately, we are told, the man's feet and ankles became strong, even though he had been lame all his life. 'He jumped up, stood on his feet, and started walking around. Then he went into the Temple with them, walking and jumping and praising God' (v 8, GNB).

This incident which, not surprisingly, filled onlookers with wonder and amazement, conjures up a picture of a man expressing his joy through spontaneous movement. The same joy is recaptured in a children's song, 'Peter and John went to pray', which you will find in *Junior Praise*. The words suggest their own actions, and might be wonderfully illustrated with flags and ribbons.

That dance is good for you has been recognised since long before biblical times, however. Anthropologists will confirm the evidence that since the dawn of time people have expressed their deepest spiritual and emotional needs and responses through this bodily activity. To paraphrase the writer of Ecclesiastes, if there has always been a time to mourn, there has certainly always been a time to dance (Ecclesiastes 3:4).

3

Dance Worship in the Past

In centuries gone by, dance was considered by many to be a normal and necessary part of the worship of God.

Dance in the Christian Church cannot, in fact, be said to have started at any particular time. It was probably inherited from both the Jewish tradition and the other diverse cultures into which Christianity spread.

As we know from observations of tribal and pagan societies, dance has always been felt to be a means of contacting and influencing unseen powers and the invisible forces of nature as personified in mythical figures like the rain god or earth mother, to whom dances were offered.

For many Christians, there was an important vision of dancing that took place in heaven, the concept that God's angels and all his blessed people dance perpetually in that other, beautiful place. This dance has been described by St Clement of Alexandria (d. 217). According to him, it was both acceptable and desirable to display physically the longing to enter into heaven during church worship. Similarly, St Ambrose (339-397) advocated that those wishing to be baptised must approach the font dancing.

There was an ancient ritual of dancing in churchyards around the tombs of martyrs. Though some Church Fathers frowned upon the practice, it had, according to Gregory of Nazianzus (329-390), three benefits: the suppression of devils, knowledge of things to come, and last, but not least, the avoidance of diseases.

On certain church festivals in the fifteenth century, the boy choristers of Seville are recorded as dancing before the high altar dressed as angels, while church processions as late as the seventeenth century included dancing. Participants are thought to have believed that to dance in honour of the saints would promote abundant harvest and cure illness.

Over the centuries, many instances of what is termed dance epidemic or choreomania have been recorded. This is when whole groups of people were regarded as being 'possessed'. Their movements, through cramps, fits and hallucinations, were described as a 'dance'.

The victims 'performed' in churches dedicated to the Virgin Mary, St John the Baptist, St Vitus and other saints, sometimes leaping high before the altar, demonstrating how they wished to receive full movement back in their afflicted limbs.

In the last quarter of the sixteenth century, it was discovered that these symptoms were caused by some sort of poisoning connected with impurities in grain, and a new sickness, ergotism, was diagnosed. It is interesting, however, that sufferers sought in actual dancing a healing of their pains, and that their search for it continued to take them, dancing, into places of worship.

From the fourth to the end of the eighteenth century, dancing in and around churches began to be prohibited. In every century, without exception, there were Christian leaders who found the practice offensive and did all they could to ban it. These included popes, archbishops, missionaries, councils and synods, representing variously the notion that the medium of dance was worldly, sinful and secular, unworthy to be used to worship God in his holy temple.

Charles and John Wesley, stressing personal holiness, had no time for Christian dance, while the established church of the eighteenth century was also inclined to look askance.

A striking exception to this attitude was the phenomenon of the eighteenth-century Shakers. They were a religious group originally formed in Manchester in 1747. Led by Mother Ann Lee, an illiterate charismatic textile worker, they found a new home in the American colonies. The Shakers' celibate fellowship thrived on sacred dance, seeing it as supported by the Scriptures, and so they recreated, in songs, and especially movements, the story of a dancing King David, the Shiloh festivals of long ago, and many other biblical stories. Their revival song 'Simple Gifts' is set to the traditional folk tune later used by Sidney Carter for his famous hymn 'Lord of the Dance'.

Victorian worship is usually depicted as very restrained, and the evidence we have from literature and other sources suggests there was little movement and much verbiage. In an era where even piano legs had to be modestly covered, and self-expression was thought in extreme bad taste, it is not surprising that many of our Victorian forefathers distrusted and feared the human body and behaved (at least in public!) as if it were somehow shameful.

Sadly, this not very wholesome example seems to linger in many of our mainstream churches today. It has resulted in a rigid style of worship that has become so habitual and ritualistic that it can seem stultifying and decidedly off-putting to the outsider.

The chequered history of Christian dance — from frenzied angel worship to sick choreomania to the repressed sexuality of our great great grandparents — means that, unlike our Hindu friends and Jewish cousins, we as Christians have no true dance tradition to pass on to our children. All we can do, with the help of God the Holy Spirit, is to dance them bravely into the future.

4

Dance – for All!

'Let's dance!' suggested the notice outside my church in the small, ex-mining village of Chadsmoor, Cannock. In this part of post-industrial Staffordshire in the late 1990s it seemed an almost ludicrous invitation — the whim, no doubt, of a certain new female vicar!

Everyone knew St Chad's as a cold building made of austere Victorian brick that people might have gone to long ago, but that nowadays was frequented by a dwindling group of old-age pensioners and a small number of children at Sunday school. Although still sought after as a venue for baptisms, weddings and funerals, St Chad's was, surely, the last place on earth where anyone would go to dance!

It is precisely through the medium of Christian dance, however, that St Chad's has found a new lease of life this past year or so, ever since its adjacent church hall became the venue for our regular Saturday afternoon sessions in what we unthreateningly describe as 'praise and worship through movement to Christian music'.

Some participants come from several miles away, while others are members of our own congregation and Sunday school. They pay a small entrance fee which goes towards the church fund, and spend three hours with a mid-afternoon break for a cold drink. We begin with prayer and a Bible reading, then some singing of popular choruses before everyone is invited to move to the centre of the room.

After gentle warm-ups as described in the back of this book, we all enjoy being taught dances which encourage us to praise God with a new confidence and spontaneity. For these sessions I am very grateful to my friends, Damien Grantley and Mavis Smith, who have not only helped teach, but have brought equipment and props in the shape of a portable cross, overhead projector, and flags and ribbons.

In the power of the Holy Spirit, Damien and Mavis have also greatly encouraged St Chad's congregation into being more open to this new and comparatively radical form of worship by dancing in a Eucharistic service. The music 'Panis angelicus' was carefully and prayerfully chosen, as was the time and place (the sermon slot at an evening service). Before the dance I spent a few moments preparing the congregation by describing the different ways of worship, and stressing that each is unique and special to God, so long as it comes from our hearts.

'Beautiful!' was the pleasing response I heard, and, 'We've never had anything like *that* before!' The atmosphere was full of surprise and delight, almost as if my small, rather traditional congregation couldn't quite believe that anyone should go to such trouble just to enhance their Sunday evening worship. That in itself was a tiny seed of a new life that I pray will grow and flourish as our church family begins to expand and welcome new members, and fresh, imaginative expressions of worship.

What is beginning to happen at St Chad's has already happened in many other churches both before and after the inception of the Christian Dance Fellowship of Britain in 1990, which is part of the International Christian Dance Fellowship which began in Australia. The CDFB is an interdenominational charity which, in the words of its constitution, 'Seeks to promote the use of dance and creative movement as an expression of the Christian faith.'

At the last count, the British fellowship has 1,000 members, though numbers are growing all the time as the Holy Spirit inspires more and more Christians to express their love of the Lord in this way. The newsletter 'Tent of David' tells many encouraging stories of work not only in churches, but across denominations and in outdoor settings such as shopping centres and arcades.

In my own experience, the strong visual impact of an outdoor dance will often make passers-by stop, whereas a preacher might have them putting down their heads and hurrying by. The spiritual value of such an outreach cannot be underestimated. The most surprising people are often moved by dance, and might be persuaded by what they see to take another look at what Jesus Christ has to offer them. There is something non-threatening and yet very moving about this form of communication.

In recent years, the Lord seems to be leading the way for those specifically called to specialisation such as youth dance, dance for men, and dance sign language for the deaf.

Youth dance

One of the chief exponents of Christian dance among young people in this country is Julia Myles, co-ordinator for the dancers of the New English Orchestra. Speaking of the way dance can be a healing medium for the troubled adolescent years, Julia says:

'I know teenagers for whom there have been precious times of release through moving before God. Issues of encouragement, acceptance, security of young people in our congregations need to be addressed, and we need to teach and draw out our young people in both expressing themselves as well as those who clearly are called and anointed to dance and minister to others.'

Teenagers have always been drawn to the kind of place where people dance, whether the quaint 'dance hall hop' of my own youth, or the more sophisticated night clubs of today. It's to do, primarily, with the music, and with being with peers, with moving in a socially acceptable way, being 'cool'.

The last thing teenagers want is to be *un*cool, embarrassed, or to look like a 'wally', and that especially applies to Christian teenagers, perhaps already sensitive through feeling 'different' to their school or college friends.

The way to avoid this, if you are lucky enough to have young, would-be dancers in your church, is to let them choose the movements and music for themselves, even though the music might seem secular and the movements jerky and unfamiliar. In 'Body and Soul', we had a group of four girls who choreographed Michael Jackson's song 'What about the Children?' and then performed it at a harvest festival service. It was a very moving and also spiritual interpretation which gave everyone a lot to think about.

At the same time, though, as Julia Myles is quick to point out, it is important not to patronise our young people who dance. 'It's a kind of tokenism on our part, but we don't always take them seriously,' she says. 'As adults we want to learn more, refine our skills, critically assess what we do in front of others, but then we say, "Ah, it's the young ones! How lovely!" As if it's somehow different for them, and anything goes because they're teenagers!'

'Let's talk and share with them!' Julia urges. 'They need to be allowed to have ideas, to be encouraged to assess their own work (just as they are in school today), and we need to assist where needed by listening and commenting, giving them tools to craft with and questions to ask. We do them a disservice and belittle their gifts and ideas with anything less!'

As in all things, balance is all important so that there is an atmosphere of trust and respect across the age divide. Teenagers need to feel both secure and affirmed before they can begin to express what is deep within them. In some church situations, the encouragement of one slightly older person who oversees what is essentially a young dance group is enough for a group to take wings.

If, however, there seems no possibility of your church teenagers ever getting beyond the 'No way am I standing up front!' mode, please don't despair.

Julia Myles assures us that while not prepared to dance, many young people *are* drawn to meditative or Celtic, reflective-style worship, even, and sometimes especially, when it means being physically involved.

'I know young people who really respond to such things as writing on and burning, screwing up or throwing paper, moulding plasticine, forming groups, gestures, even eating chips! These have been part of the work of Birmingham Diocese Youth Worship initiative, with co-ordinator, Nick Wills. I see this as very important, non-cringey introductions to the importance of using our bodies and recognising ourselves as a "whole" involved in worship, not just our spirit or our mind.'

In 1997, Julia circulated a youth dance questionnaire for the eleven to twenty-fives, and also one for youth dance leaders. The results make interesting reading. Out of 62 responses, 30 said they perform in church, 15 in theatres, 9 in school, 6 in outreach and another 6 in the street. Styles ranged from ballet (15) to tap (14), modern (13), worship (11), with stage/jazz at 9 and expressive (5) further down the popularity scale.

According to the survey, many are totally committed to Christ and feel called to use dance, mime and other creative arts as an expression of worship. It should also be noted, remembering Julia's comments on how teenagers are sometimes treated in our churches, that they take training very seriously, often having technique classes in several styles.

Most encouragingly, nearly all the teenagers stressed the therapeutic value of being able to express their feelings in dance, and a large number find a sense of acceptance and well-being through movement, particularly when it is directed towards God.

As one young dancer succinctly put it, 'I can use the whole of my body to worship the guy who made it!'

Men's dance

'Just so long as you don't expect *me* to do it!' is what the usually senior male church wardens always say. But one of the most heartening things happening to Christian dance in the past few years is the number of men who are being used by the Lord in this very special ministry.

Andy Raine (who looks more like a bricklayer than the ballet dancer he assures me he isn't!) told a CDFB conference how at weekly fellowship meetings he always wanted to worship with his whole being. But he was always aware that he was definitely the 'wrong build'.

'I had too much height and not enough weight, but if God could use me as I was, I was at least available,' he says in his book *I Will Be With You*. 'Moses had a stammer, and when God called him, he replied, "Here I am — send my brother instead!" God had work for both of them.'

Andy's no-nonsense, 'blokey' approach to dance has, over the years, encouraged many other men to forget their preconceived ideas and join or form groups, and male membership of the fellowship is now growing steadily. Some of these new members are trained male dancers who happen to be Christians, or those who have pursued some kind of dancing as a hobby and found the Lord calling them to use their skills in a new dimension.

But for every Christian dance man who, like Damien Grantley, was once headed for a professional career in musical comedy, there is at least another who is like Albert Wilkinson, a middle-aged family man who found himself dancing for the Lord almost by accident.

As circuit steward for the Dudley and Netherton Methodist Circuit, part of Albert's job was to read and distribute notices of forthcoming events. When, in 1995, he heard that 'Body and Soul' was holding a workshop day, he decided to go along, taking his wife and young son and daughter with him.

'The whole family is interested in drama,' Albert explains, 'and we thought we might be doing some characterisation and mime, which would help in church productions. I don't think any of us expected to be dancing, especially me, but once we started, we were hooked!'

Over the next two years, the Wilkinsons made a wonderful contribution to the group, and Albert's talent for improvisation often added an extra dimension to our interpretations. For his ten-year-old son, Philip, he was a great example, and it was a delight to see the family moving together in worship that was also energetic, dramatic and fun.

Dance *is* dramatic, and it is a fairly safe bet that people who are already involved in church drama groups will be kindly disposed towards it. Choirs and choral societies might also have wanted to add a bit of movement to their productions but not known how to start. So if you're looking for would-be dancers, male or female, these might well be the places to look.

You may find one or two men who are willing to come along occasionally to add weight to a particular event or performance without making the commitment to a regular session. But don't make the mistake I once saw in a theological college service where one man had obviously volunteered, or been coerced into playing the part of Jesus, and then was left, arms painfully outstretched for ten minutes, while everyone else danced around him!

Men, particularly when they are completely inexperienced in dance, can be notoriously diffident, or, what is worse, extremely derisive about this form of worship. It's all about being vulnerable and showing emotions, things which men are still not brought up to deal with very well.

The dance teacher Margaret Stevens, who started the famous St Michael Dancers in Coventry Cathedral writes about once being involved with the in-service training of Church of England clergy. On one occasion she was faced with a group of sixteen men from inner-city parishes, none of whom had danced before. One, who looked like a Welsh rugby player, said, 'If you ask me to do press-ups, I will.'

'They were,' she said, 'probably the shyest group I ever had,' but the fact that she was over fifty, non threatening — and had rugby-playing sons — helped them to relax and enjoy themselves.

It helped to call what they did movement rather than dance, as this seemed less frightening. Since they knew the Bible, Margaret concludes, it was but a small step to translate into movement words like 'then shall the eyes of the blind be opened, and the ears of the deaf unstopped'.*

As with teenagers, it is important to remember to let the Holy Spirit direct the movements that come most naturally. Men look and feel silly imitating the delicate gestures that very often come more easily to women. The still centre that they move from within must be one they discover for themselves, for then they will find a strength and a grace which brings its own balance and dignity.

Dance signing for the deaf

British sign language classes have become extremely popular over recent years. It's surprising just how many people are learning this vital and rather beautiful means of silent communication. The impact of signing came home to me forcibly some months ago when a clergy colleague of mine, a young woman priest who happens to be profoundly deaf, interpreted a prayer poem at one of our staff team residentials.

As usual, there had been a lot of debate and even more hot air during the day as the busy, 'Martha-like' Church of England seemed to whisk us about being professional and important. Then, suddenly, there was Hannah, who thankfully also lip-reads very well, spelling out anguished words about silence and listening, her mobile hands mouthing the wisdom Mary might have been lucky enough to catch at Jesus' feet.

For me, personally, the debates and deliberations of that

---

* Margaret Stevens, *A Bounty of Passing Moments*, p 17.

conference have long been forgotten. But the memory of the expressive sign language remains, as both an encouragement and a warning. How much valuable time we do spend, listening to the sound of our own voices!

'Dance signing' is, to my knowledge, a fairly new phenomenon, and one that is sweeping the Christian dance scene. The signs are made, but with exaggeration, concentration being given to the wordless vocabulary of worship.

The chief exponent in the Christian Dance Fellowship is Linda Wells, who has recently moved to America. She described graphically how she felt God was calling her to learn signing, as many people are currently being called. She didn't know why, until a deaf friend came to her church one Sunday.

'He asked me if I would stand up and "sign" one of the hymns for him,' she said. 'I didn't really want to do it, but I'm so glad I did! My friend just stood there, staring, with the tears rolling down his cheeks! He said it was the first time he had ever been able to "listen" to a hymn in his whole life! I've been teaching Christian signing ever since!'

Dance signing is not only beneficial to the observer. Hand and finger signals can be used effectively to help disabled and elderly people to worship in movement. For instance, a simple chorus like 'Thank you, Jesus!' can be transformed when the sedentary singers are encouraged to 'sign' its very special meaning. Even one or two small movements can say so very much.

Signing is also a very good start for anyone who feels called to dance, but feels inhibited by their lack of movement vocabulary. Although some dancers have perfected it so that they seem to 'chatter' with their hands while travelling with their feet, most dance signers are content to stay fairly stationary, creating their interpretations gently and beautifully with their hands, making intercession in a very special way.

5

Those Who Couldn't - Did!

No matter how awkward you feel, how ill equipped and totally untrained, it's wonderful to know that the Lord *can* use you to dance for him. He can set you free in a new and special way to express your love and help your faith to grow.

Just to encourage you, I've included a few 'case histories' of people whose lives have been changed by using their bodies to praise the Lord.

The hit and run victim

Jenny is a teenager who, twelve months before I knew her, had been knocked off her skateboard in the street by a hit-and-run driver who later tried to set fire to the car. Jenny suffered brain damage, and for several weeks lay in a coma. The whole church community prayed for her, but it seemed she had little chance of survival, let alone recovery.

When, miraculously, she did regain consciousness, she was a different girl. Her speech was slurred, her vision impaired. Clumsy and unco-ordinated, she had to relive and relearn all her development from babyhood.

When she was brought along by two other teenage girls to 'Body and Soul', Jenny at first sat out. She was noisy and disruptive, and prone to temper tantrums. But she was so full of spontaneous affection when the tantrums died down, we all felt we had to hug and forgive her.

One night, as we sat quietly at our prayers, asking for the help and guidance of the Holy Spirit before we began to dance, Jenny suddenly blurted out: 'I prayed I'd die after the accident! I don't know why that man had to do this to me!'

We prayed many times for healing for Jenny, and it came, as we hoped, through the dance. Gradually, she realised she was among friends who weren't going to laugh at her, and tentatively, she began to join in.

Jenny's confidence grew as her co-ordination improved. It was a very proud moment when her mother came to see her take part in a church service, dancing to the hymn 'Holy, Holy, Holy' on Ascension Day, with five other worshippers of all ages, sizes and abilities.

'I don't hate that man who knocked me down any more,' she told me quietly, before we went home. 'My mum had told me not to go out on the skateboard, but I only just remembered that!'

If there was one turning point in Jenny's story, that was it.

The man with no legs

'Look, vicar, I'm doing my exercises!' said the ninety-year-old man with no legs.

Although Ben couldn't walk, he spent at least a couple of hours each day in therapeutic movement. Using his still strong arms and upper torso to pull himself upright on the cot-sided bed, he took a small, hard cushion and 'knelt' on it so that it took his weight. His intention was to harden the stumps that he hoped would eventually take his weight, and also to keep the rest of his body in trim so that he didn't get fat!

To Ben, a committed Christian, those daily exercises were a lifeline, his dedication to them worthy of any athlete. Telling me the story of how his legs were amputated as a result of diabetes, he said he believed the Lord had spared him, even without legs, for a purpose, and he praised and thanked him every day.

'I've told the doctor I'm going to have artificial legs one day,' he told me on one of my visits to the nursing home where he lived. 'All I need is to get my balance back!'

Sadly, that was never to be because Ben died before he could achieve his aim of walking again. But he had been an inspiration to many, including the doctor who visited him, and everyone knew what had kept him going so long after most people would have given up.

It was, quite simply, the discipline of those daily movements, movements which, in their own way, had brought hope and a special kind of Christian healing.

Like a prisoner of war I once heard of, who walked around the world in his imagination as he paced the narrow confines of his cell, Ben was able to look beyond the cold reality of his mutilated physical body to the wholeness that comes from being one with Christ.

'If the son sets you free, you will be free indeed' (John 8:36).

Marie and Andrew's story

Marie Bensley, Bristol and West joint co-ordinator of the Christian Dance Fellowship of Britain, tells the remarkable story of how God used dance to heal her marriage and lead her and her husband Andrew into a whole new life.

The story began with a tragedy when Marie's eighteen-year-old son by a previous marriage died very suddenly from an unsuspected heart defect. Young Alistair's death hit Andrew particularly hard, and because Marie was trying to cope with her own grief (her mother died just a month after Alistair), she did not quite realise the depth of the depression Andrew was suffering. Work became more and more important to him, their faith in God was affected, and, almost inevitably, a marriage that had been so happy began to fall apart at the seams.

'We had started counselling,' Marie recounts, 'but that opened more wounds. Reaching an all-time low in 1992, they decided to go, as they usually did, to Spring Harvest. It would be an attempt at reconciliation neither really expected to be fruitful.

'We went to the Big Top for the evening celebration,' Marie goes on. 'Two hurting, damaged people not really wanting to be there, and not really enjoying the lively praise and worship.'

It was then that the singing group began teaching the worshippers a new song, 'You have broken the chains', a song all about Jesus' victory over death, and onto the stage leapt Andy Au, a dark-haired young man with slightly oriental features.

'At the words, "You have broken the chains," he pulled a wooden stave down onto his bowed shoulders,' Marie remembers. 'He danced with such passion, such feeling, such energy, his face contorted with the pain expressed in the words of the song, and that dance and that song went straight to my husband's heart.'

The Holy Spirit used Andy's powerful dance to release Marie and Andrew from the weight of bereavement, to begin to heal their marriage, and to give them a totally unexpected new start in life.

Marie, wanting to learn more about Christian dance, booked herself into an international conference taking place in York, and while there, heard the Lord telling her to share the testimony of what had happened at Spring Harvest.

Meanwhile, Andrew was being interviewed for a new job that would take the couple from London to a less stressful, more spiritually rewarding environment in Somerset.

'I thought I would teach in Somerset,' Marie takes up the story, 'but the Lord had other ideas and I found myself being used more and more in the Christian dance world. Andrew has also become involved, and helps run their monthly dance workshops at Taunton and Watchett.

'Since York 1994, we both want to dance for the Lord, and plan to continue dancing our story to bring healing and hope to others hurting in this world.'

Fiona, the dancer who died

There is a circle dance called 'Christ as a light', based loosely on St Patrick's Breastplate, which was taught some years ago to a group of CDFB members by Fiona Bennett.

It is now usually performed in her honour because Fiona, who was just twenty-eight years old, died peacefully on 14 April 1996. At the beginning of November 1995 she had been diagnosed with leukaemia.

Fiona loved to dance, and her final presentation dance was before the Archbishop of Canterbury, George Carey, during his visit to the Diocese of Worcester in October 1995.

In a letter written days before she died, Fiona wrote to thank her friends and fellow dancers for their prayers, and to encourage us that the Lord had protected her against much suffering. She referred to a Scripture passage which had been given to her some years before, and now had special meaning: 'But for you who revere my name, the sun of righteousness will rise with healing in its wings. And you will go out and leap like calves, released from the stall' (Malachi 4:2).

A short time before Fiona's death, her church fellowship received a beautiful 'picture' of her leaving her earthly body and dancing with the Lord. A reminder that for every one of us, ultimate, eternal healing is only possible in God's heavenly kingdom.

There are many other stories which could be told. A lifelong dancer, crippled after a back injury, now runs a Christian dance group and reports: 'Since I have been dancing for the Lord, I have been pain free.'

Another lady, who suffers from depression, is helped by merely imagining herself dancing freely in God's Spirit. Yet another describes being first called to dance when she was in a neck collar, having suffered back and neck problems for many years.

'I was told I would have to wear a collar for the rest of my life. This was twelve years ago, and I am now a very fit, energetic member of the church dance group and have led children's and juniors' dance classes for the past eight years.' She adds that it is not just physical but emotional healing that she has experienced.

Courage and determination obviously play a part in these healings. People feel called to move in worship even when moving hurts or seems impossible. And they persevere, dancing against the odds.

Such people speak of being given a new start, having their lives saved, and in one case I came across this is literally true.

On Christmas Eve 1997, a young American woman found herself stranded on a mountain ski area in Utah, and had to spend more than eighteen hours alone in freezing conditions. When finally rescued by helicopter the next day, she attributed her miraculous survival to the fact that she had systematically sung — and danced — through every hymn she had ever known!

6

Keep on Dancing!

Some Hints and Practical Advice

Private dance devotion

As previously mentioned, there is nothing wrong with dancing alone in worship. For some people it is less threatening and more fulfilling than to join a group.

In my experience, however, the most difficult thing about dancing before the Lord in private is actually setting aside a time each day that you can give wholly to him. Your intentions are good. Tomorrow you'll begin, when there's more time and space, and you've less on your mind. Or next week, when you're on holiday, you'll make a brand-new start. All you really need, after all, is a new daily routine.

On that last point, you are absolutely right. Most schedules, whether you're at home or out at work, can be altered to accommodate half an hour of daily private dance worship. The secret is in selecting the half an hour from the right portion of your day.

My own experience as a busy parish priest is that no matter how good my intentions, dancing in worship first thing in the morning does not work. I might manage it one day a week (usually on my day off!) but for the rest of the time there are school assemblies, Eucharists in church, and staff meetings which all take place around nine o'clock.

Similarly, in the evenings, there are meetings, baptism visits and wedding rehearsals all taking place just at the time when most other people are following their leisure pursuits.

Allowing for the fact that it's always advisable never to

exercise on a full stomach, there did not seem to be any suitable half hours in my busy day. And yet, I wanted so badly to praise God with my body in this way! *Not* being able to just made me grumpy and frustrated, a state which, luckily, brought me to prayer.

'Show me the right time, Lord,' I asked, as I emerged, emotionally battered, from a hurried ten minutes with my tape player. 'This just isn't good enough for you!'

A couple of days later, I arrived home from a sick communion visit which had been preceded by a big funeral, to find the latter part of the afternoon almost miraculously clear.

At seven I had baptism preparation, and at eight was meeting a couple to rehearse their wedding. But now it was only four thirty!

'What do I usually do at four thirty?' I asked myself, and already knew the answer. I sat down with the local paper and a cup of tea and took a break before our household prayers and evening meal.

So surely, the voice of the Holy Spirit was whispering to me, *this* was the time I had available for my private dance worship! It was a naturally quiet time as far as the telephone was concerned, and though you can never be completely sure in a vicarage, the doorbell was more likely to ring after tea than before it. An added bonus was that dancing at this time kept me away from the biscuits which all too often accompanied my afternoon 'cuppa', and it also provided a much needed boost to my physical, emotional and spiritual batteries.

For me, this afternoon time works really well. If I'm lucky I can get in a whole hour of dance worship and my body and my spirit has now come to look forward to it and rely upon its beneficial results.

For you, the afternoon may be impossible, particularly if you are not able to work from home, or you have children coming in from school. But no matter how busy and hard pressed you are, I do urge you to ask the Lord to show you the best time in your day. The time he is already waiting for you to spend with him in dance worship.

It may be first thing in the morning, before the family gets up, or last thing at night before you fall, still praising him, into bed. It might even be half an hour before lunch, if you are able to go home, or find some other private place. The important thing is to relax and enjoy being in his company knowing you won't be interrupted. (For this purpose, an answerphone is a wonderful asset, as is a husband who is prepared to head off unexpected visitors and also start cooking the tea while you dance!)

Dancing alone obviously has a different dynamic than dancing with others. You need a room which is warm and well ventilated, with a bit of space, and obviously room to keep your player and tapes.

Bedrooms are perfect, especially if they happen to be no longer occupied by grown-up children who won't mind you moving the furniture around a bit. Visual aids, such as a cross on the wall or on a table, and candles are good for atmosphere, and if you want to 'check' your movements, a lot can be done with a big, discarded dressing table mirror attached to the main wall with hooks and strong rope. A foam or camping-type mat that's long enough to lie on is useful for meditation and warm-up exercises, but not compulsory.

Make sure you're wearing something loose and your feet are comfortable, either bare or in ballet shoes or socks. Then light your candle, and moving into the most comfortable position for you, spend some time in prayer. If it helps, play some quiet instrumental music as you ask the Lord to receive the praise and worship you are about to offer him as a declaration of your love. Ask him to free you so that you can express that love from the very bottom of your heart.

Next, depending on the amount of time available, use the relaxation technique, and definitely the 'warm-up' routine in the back of this book before changing your music again to accommodate your dance. The most important thing about the music you choose for private devotion is that it inspires, uplifts or quietens you, so that you can give it back to God, as something that one way or another delights, as he delights in each one of us.

It seems silly to say that you can feel embarrassed dancing on your own but I know from my own experience that it's true. So the first thing to remember as you self-consciously raise an arm or move a leg is that this isn't strange and it will get easier. One of the really great things about dancing in private is that you don't have to compare your movements with anyone else's.

Try and move spontaneously to your music, if that comes easily, or work out steps to a solo dance, playing one of your special songs over and over until it is choreographed to your own liking, and you can write down the steps in a book if you want to use them again. As you dance, try and visualise Jesus looking down on you, smiling his approval, warming you with his love.

This time is very precious, to him as well as to you. It is a time when, in my experience, the Lord will very often choose to speak, to solve a problem or to make a suggestion that will come directly through the medium of the movement, so that I will catch my breath and be newly inspired. And that refreshing inspiration is all I need to face the rest of my day, however long or potentially stressful it happens to be.

Dancing your prayers

A woman in my congregation was very angry with God because, to her mind, he cruelly let her twin brother die twenty years before. When she came to the altar to receive communion, she showed God her anger by keeping her hands and arms tightly at her side while those around her lifted theirs for the blessed sacrament. Only at the very last minute did Dora give way, jerking her hands reluctantly into the accepted posture, receiving the elements with the air of one who has made her point and is now ready to conform.

Expressing our prayers in movement is nothing new; indeed the whole liturgy of the Eucharist is built upon action as much as the spoken word. We stand for the hymns and for the Gospel reading. We sit for the sermon and, depending on our tradition, kneel to pray.

Leading the service, I am always aware of this — sensing how important is the choreography between, say, server and those who bring up the offertory gifts. In my rather high church tradition, each responsive bow is made for a reason, and at exactly the right moment.

Praying, especially praying for other people, can, therefore, seem restrictive and uninspiring from a fixed position. We find it hard, if not impossible, to know what to ask for because, realistically, we cannot feel what the other person feels or be sure of their needs, and if we are required to do it uncomfortably on our knees, or leading stiffly from a lectern, it is sometimes hard to receive the Holy Spirit's messages.

It is in this context that intercessory dance can be both liberating and valuable, enabling us, by opening ourselves to the Holy Spirit, to use our imaginations as well as our bodies to make pleas and petitions on behalf of others.

Unless a church is used to dance worship, it is probably best to explore this form of prayer in the safety of the dance group meeting to begin with. It is important that participants feel comfortable and are able to express themselves freely so that they can intercede silently for others — that is, in movement — without feeling foolish.

A good way to start is with total relaxation and then to ask each person as and when they are ready, to move gently to the Taizé chant 'O Lord, hear my prayer', or some other gentle music, at the same time interpreting in simple movements what they feel may be the need of someone on their hearts.

As always, it is important to stress that there is no compunction, and if a person just wishes to sit and gently think of someone who is sick or otherwise in need, they are free to do so.

The beauty of intercessory dance is that at its best it is true empathy. Nothing can bring you closer to a person than physically to bring their problem before the Lord, feeling in your own body the pain of their depression, fear or loneliness, or the aching of their limbs as they drag them around.

Only God knows the full extent of their true needs, however, and so it is important to ask him to show you some of the hidden tensions that may lie beneath the surface (eg Dora's behaviour was due to her lingering bereavement). It is also naturally just as vital to follow up your prayers by not only telling the subject you are praying for them, but by showing a kind and friendly interest in their future welfare.

The Lord's Prayer

'Saying' the Lord's Prayer through dance can be very powerful and uplifting. A new and even deeper meaning is given to the familiar words Jesus taught his disciples as we try to interpret them with our bodies.

For us at 'Exercise in Prayer' and later, 'Body and Soul', the prayer was a natural progression from our verbal opening prayers which we said around our floor candle in the quietness of the peaceful church. It also seems to have a very positive response from the primary school children I come into contact with in parish ministry.

There are several versions (one reproduced in the resources) but the one I use is slow and sweeping, starting in a kneeling position and progressing upwards and outward on words like 'power' and 'glory', and ending as it begins, with the hands held as for prayer.

It can be sung unaccompanied, or the words slowly read by one person, or said by the whole group. Its beauty lies in the fact that it is known by all, and therefore unthreatening when presented as a dance prayer. People can close their eyes or use the dance to illustrate their petitions mentally. They can move as much or as little as they like in accompaniment, and not leave their pews unless they really want to.

'The Lord's Prayer' has great power when presented in a service, and can be a good introduction when a congregation is nervous or uncertain about the place of dance in their worship.

Congregational dance

Persuading your congregation to move might not be as difficult as you think. As previously stated, movement is already present to one degree or another — people usually stand to sing a hymn, listen to the Gospel and to say the Creed; they may kneel or stand to pray, may bow to the altar in acknowledgement of the presence of God, or cross themselves in response to the absolution and blessing; they may bring their hands together in front of the heart or over the face for intercessory prayer, or raise their hands in praise.

Many of these movements are instinctive, and the last thing you want is to make people self-conscious about them. But their enhancement can bring a new awareness that will deepen spirituality and make worship more meaningful, as people are encouraged to meditate on the true meaning of what they are doing with their bodies.

This may be accomplished simply by the worship leader going through the gestures slowly and prayerfully, indicating their power and significance even when it seems blatantly obvious — eg 'When we raise our hands like this, we are showing God just how great we think he is', or 'When we make the sign of the cross on our bodies, we are remembering what Jesus did by dying for us.'

Such an exercise, perhaps in a sermon slot, might well give new confidence to a congregation which teeters on the brink of movement, and gives people permission to move (though it should be clearly stated they don't *have* to!).

For some churches, with fixed furniture and even more inflexible members, the exploration of symbolic movement in the pew might be as far as you can go. Others, with more user-friendly buildings, movable chairs and carpeted areas, might be persuaded to take part in congregational dancing as part of the service.

If you feel the Holy Spirit might be leading your fellowship in that direction, then pray about it. Enlist the support of your worship leader, and go for something simple so that everyone who wishes to can join in.

A beautiful yet very simple congregational Christmas dance is one set to 'Silent Night' which you will find in the resources section. This is a spiral dance which needs little skill and no experience and yet can be very effective, especially if candles are used. Do try it if there is room in your church to make a circle of people.

For some churches, the nearest thing to dance is procession. And there is nothing wrong with that. One large inner-city parish church I know of uses part of the Good Friday liturgy for a procession all the way round the inside of the building. The pilgrim congregation moves at its own pace, matching steps and voices to the strains of the old Easter hymns which seem to swell from every side. Pauses are made in the Lady chapel, by the font, and in the west end before the procession goes down through the nave to the cross, which is laid down at the foot of the chancel steps. Even before the moment when each participant venerates the cross with a touch or a kiss, there is not a dry eye in the house.

At the same church, a children's worship service on the morning of Good Friday traditionally ends with the youngsters joining hands and singing 'Lord of the Dance' as they make their own skipping procession outside and right round the building.

Both services are talked about long afterwards, each celebrating in its own way but with movement at its heart, and gradually becoming part of the Easter liturgy of that particular church, and making it even more special.

Processions are special — grand and dramatic — and should be made the very most of, so if you are blessed with an ancient, atmospheric building, start to think about marching, and, if possible, using flags and ribbons. For many congregations it's the nearest they will come to dancing, and the excitement is just as authentic and the offering every bit as precious to God.

Another way to get a congregation to move is with the blessing at the end of your service. For some, just saying the grace holding hands can be a very powerful experience, something that may be built on at a later date by the introduction of a chorus like 'Bind us together', sung with linked arms. For examples of other blessings see resources section.

Dance as play

I hadn't played hopscotch for over forty years until the Saturday I went to a dance day at a church near Stourbridge!

'We're all going to *play!*' explained Jane Grimshaw, one of the organisers, as a group of all ages and sizes came into the empty church. Empty, that is, except for huge, multi-coloured piles of toys. 'There are balls, skipping ropes, bean bags, dressing-up shawls — oh, everything you can think of! Today we're going to praise God by letting him hear us giggle like little children again!'

It was, to say the least, a novel idea. But also, I suddenly realised, quite an appealing one. Especially to someone like me, a team vicar with Certain Responsibilities. So I took off my coat and hung it, toddler like, on the floor.

Then I stood and watched as other grown-up children came in and stared open mouthed at what lay before them. With the maypole-like, bright confusion of ribbons and colourful plastic, Christchurch, Lye, was truly transformed into one vast, safe and beautiful nursery floor!

The few inhibitions that hung around soon gave way. Within moments we were all playing with gusto, tossing bean bags and balls, dressing up in the beautiful, trailing scarves and shawls that had been piled beneath the sanctuary cross. Unwinding a communal skipping rope, and turning it in a unison that invited any passer-by to run in and skip.

Discovering the hopscotch — big, plastic discs in orange, yellow, blue and red — took me straight back across those forty odd years to the pavement chalk and pebble games of my childhood. As I threw the beanbag marker and began to hop (discovering how difficult it was!) I heard an enormous cheer!

In the midst of an admiring group, a woman kept not one, not two, but three hula hoops spinning around herself. While in other parts of the noisy building, others thoroughly enjoyed playing 'I'm the king of the castle!' or hand ball.

If, as our leader had said, God really did want to hear us giggle, he certainly wasn't disappointed that day. But as we later discovered, our 'play workshop' did have a serious dimension, and it was all to do with thanks and praise.

'Listen to the music, and then offer back to God your happy memories of childhood,' we were invited, as one by one, we flopped down to recover from our busy playtime. 'Then gather up your favourite toys and take them to the cross.'

We were also asked to give to our heavenly Father those childhood memories that were perhaps not so happy, the painful things we had perhaps not been able to acknowledge or relinquish until now, and there were counsellors on hand to minister to those in need of special healing prayers.

Gradually, the little clusters of dancers began to move, gathering up balls and trinkets and carrying them carefully into the sanctuary and the huge, waiting cross. Many stayed there thoughtfully, making an impromptu tableau amid the confusion and the grace.

Bowed, silent figures at the foot of the cross, recreating the image of those other figures, long, long ago. And a voice, drawing memories of nurture and childhood from each one of us.

'Woman, behold thy son. Son, behold thy mother.'

A day to be remembered and to cherish. Perhaps your group might be led by the Holy Spirit in the same direction some time.

If you really can't dance — watch!

For some people, getting up to dance will never be possible. They may be too old, or ill, or handicapped. They may simply be too shy even to consider moving around in worship. But that does not mean they are unable either to participate in or benefit from the healing qualities of Christian dance.

A very arthritic lady, watching a graceful dancer, explained how she was dancing too, 'on the inside' as she watched, while another friend tells the story of how, asked to speak at a pensioners' club, she felt called to present a dance, a simple solo about her own personal relationship with Jesus.

For this dance, she draped a rocking chair with colourful cloth, and placed a crown on the last, purple velvet layer, thus transforming it into a throne for him. When her dance ended, with her laying her head, and her burdens, on the 'lap' of the throne, she realised that many of the elderly ladies watching her were in tears.

They had found her interpretation so moving, the realistic 'props' making them powerfully aware of the presence of the Lord among them that afternoon.

'It made me think of a sad time I had when I lost my baby, just after the war. I really needed to put my head on Jesus' shoulder then,' one confided, while several confessed that they, too, had been unexpectedly moved by very poignant, private memories of their own, mostly of times when they had needed to call on Jesus in a particular way.

Dance is a language, and because it communicates without

words it can reach those emotions we all think we success-fully repress, and by reawakening them, it encourages us to re-present them at the foot of the cross.

For this, it is sometimes even better to watch someone else than physically to take part, because it is obviously less threat-ening, and the whole interpretation is visible and meaning-ful.

By the power of the imagination, we can all mentally move with the dancers we watch, entering with our minds into the spirit of what they are trying to interpret, even if our bodies are unable or unwilling to co-operate.

And sometimes it is the most unexpected, seemingly unskilled dancers who move and encourage and heal us most of all. I am thinking of a dance conference where, although a beautiful young ballerina had just faultlessly performed, it was the worship of one brave, rather lumpy middle-aged lady who brought tears to people's eyes.

Standing there on the stage in front of a couple of hundred dancers, she simply raised her eyes and her hands to the Lord, her simple steps speaking volumes because they were full of sincerity and love. And in those moments, she carried the homage of all our hearts.

7

Some Common Problems and How to Solve Them

Pews

Whether we like them or not, fixed pews are a feature of many of our inherited church buildings, and it is not always possible or even practical for them to be removed to make a church more 'dance friendly'. The best solution I have found is to work in the aisles using flags and ribbons, and to keep things moving, so that your dance has the dramatic elements of a procession and there is always something for the congregation to see, wherever they happen to be seated. This is not as difficult as it may sound, particularly if your church happens to be a Gothic 'barn' with several aisles. There needs to be plenty of colour and movement, with all the participants being encouraged to 'think cathedral' and move with dignity between the people who, to add to the effect, can always be invited to stand as if for a blessing and to sing along to the lyrics. The important thing is to try and see your particular church building in a positive rather than negative light, and pray for the insight to use it most imaginatively and worshipfully.

Visibility

This can also be a major problem. There is nothing more frustrating, for dancers and congregation alike, than to realise that what is being done is just not being seen. Again because of the design and furnishings of some churches, the chancel is just invisible from the back of the building, and the chancel is where most dances traditionally take place.

The first, obvious thing to do is check whether the church has a platform or staging stored away somewhere which would raise the area and make visibility easier. Needless to say, make sure that this is safe, and big enough for any movements, remembering that dance always takes up more room than you might originally think.

Alternatively, if there is a small congregation, you might persuade them to actually sit in the choir stalls or move closer to the front of the church (not always as easy as it sounds, as most ministers know!).

Don't lie down or kneel as part of a dance if you even suspect visibility might be a problem. You'll disappear completely from view, and what is worse, might even cause giggles as you do so.

Do practise, taking into account pews, large eagle lecterns, and other treasures not designed to dance around. Move what you can, but remember to replace them afterwards, and be extra careful not to give offence. Very often, rather unlovely items of church furniture have been given in memory of people, and often still have family connections within the church community.

Music

Many a good interpretation has been ruined by unsuitable music. You know how it is — a certain Christian song has special meaning for you, and you think how great it would be to use it in a dance. But before you do, stop and think!

The first thing to ask yourself is, are the words really clear? Many worship songs, sadly, aren't, especially if they have a lot of backing, are recorded live, or feature someone with a soft, dreamy voice.

In order that the congregation can fully appreciate, let alone enter into what you are doing, listening needs to be effortless. Better to choose another song, one with a strong beat and immediately compelling voice, either male or female, interpreting instantly audible, clearly understandable lyrics.

Always practise beforehand to get volume and tone right, and make sure the person in charge of the music isn't dancing and that they know the exact moment when to switch on and off. To avoid technical hitches, all too easy when you are nervous, record your song, on its own, on both sides of a tape, then if the wrong side gets inadvertently fed into the player, nothing is lost.

Another important point about music. Don't dismiss secular songs as being unsuitable for worship. 'Love changes everything' has more than one meaning, and the very end of Paul McCartney's 'Standing Stones' is a very powerful, spiritual piece without being overtly Christian. Both are featured in the resource section of this book.

Opposition

Some people will never accept dance in church. They either think it worldly, silly or just unnecessary, and may make no bones about telling you so. If you come up against this open hostility all you can do is respect their opinions and try not to be pushy or threatening, and, of course, never stop praying for them. There *will* come an opportunity for your group to dance if it is truly God's will for your church, but you need to use tact and diplomacy and not bombard the opposition with your ministry.

Sometimes, a specially arranged 'spot' of about three minutes, involving classical music and graceful dancers will be all that's needed to convince the opposition that what you're proposing is not so bad, after all. In other situations, it might be that what is deemed unacceptable for adults might well be tolerated and even enjoyed when performed by children. So it might be worth taking a look at what the Sunday school is currently studying, and seeing if some of it might be taught through movement and dramatic mime.

Isolation

'Dance is holy!' declares Margaret Stevens in her book *A Bounty of Passing Moments* (p. 8). You might agree whole-heartedly. But what if there is just no one in your church who is prepared to share this particular expression of holiness with you even though worship is otherwise fairly free? You stand and fidget during the choruses, longing to move beyond the holding up of 'holy hands' and yet not daring to, afraid to look silly, not wanting to draw attention to yourself.

WHY? In such a situation, when the Lord is telling you clearly to dance, you have, I suggest, only one alternative, and that is to do it! I know of several people who belong to charismatic yet non-dancing churches and yet who still dance in services, unobtrusively, at the back.

Kathryn, a young CDFB member, dances with the flags and ribbons she has used to teach her pack of Brownies, weaving colour and movement into the service at her local worship centre.

'Everyone accepts it now, although I got some strange looks at first,' she says, 'And once or twice, another lady has actually got up and joined in!'

When Kathryn was baptised by total immersion a couple of years ago, the song that was specially chosen for her was 'Teach me to dance to the beat of your heart'.

Another dancer who moves alone, conscious only of the need to worship God in this way, is Andrew, who has been training in all kinds of dance for thirteen years, and whose church is a Methodist chapel in Lichfield, Staffordshire. Andrew reports that everyone is used to his dancing during the hymns now, and that he sees it as part of his witness and ministry. He hopes, one day, to be a candidate for the

Methodist ministry, so here, praise God, we have another dancing pastor in the making! May he be one of many!

What to wear

This can be a problem, especially if your group comprises all ages. Long, swirly skirts and angel wing tops may suit some members, but your teenagers would rather die than wear them.

Similarly, leggings and T-shirts are fine on some figures, but just look horrendous on others, while traditional 'liturgical dance' outfits of all in one trouser suits or floaty white dresses can appear dated and rather overblown.

The answer lies, I am sure, in comfort and in colour. All members of the group can be given the choice as to what feels most comfortable, and just a basic colour, or colour scheme decided upon.

In 'Body and Soul's performance for 'One World Week' some wore red tops and white skirts or trousers, and others white tops with red skirts or trousers. People brought their own clothes, or borrowed, and nothing new had to be bought.

On another occasion, we all wore black, and added a simple sash of deep coral around our waists. Again, this felt effective without being too extravagant, and the male members were able to wear the same 'costume'.

The final word on dress has to be about modesty. I recently attended a Holy Communion service with some elderly members of my own congregation. Although the liturgy was beautiful, and the atmosphere very prayerful, all my companions could talk about on the way home (and for several days afterwards!) was the fact that a teenage server had been allowed to 'set up' the altar beforehand wearing, not a server's robe, but her own clothes, which unfortunately consisted of a very short, very tight and low-cut dress. The scandalised comment was that she looked as if she were wearing a swimsuit, and nobody could quite work out why!

Perhaps such a reaction might not happen in *your* church, but it is still important to be careful not to give offence. Leotards and lycra are definitely for the gym or leisure centre and on the whole look out of place in church. It's also a good idea to avoid other outfits which might draw attention to nipples or underwear lines as these things can really detract from what you are trying to achieve.

A good general rule is always to try to ensure no one in the group causes embarrassment or confusion by what they wear to dance in church. If in doubt, meet up and have a trying-on session a couple of weeks beforehand, and be honest with each other about what looks best.

What to wear on the feet depends again on comfort, and also on the practicalities of where you are dancing. Carpet can be hard on bare feet, causing actual burns; ballet shoes are not to everyone's taste, and are also quite expensive; socks are sometimes useful if a church is cold, or its floors inhospitable, but they can slip and are not always ideal to dance in.

One tip about footwear is that if you are performing everyone should ideally wear the same. So look out for light canvas shoes. You can still get those flat, black ballerina-type ones with a tiny bow on the front, and quite sturdy and flexible soles.

Avoid jewellery as this can not only be distracting, it can be dangerous.

PART TWO

RESOURCES

1   Relaxation/Meditations

2   Warm-up/Exercises

3   Simple Christian 'Signing' in Dance

4   Dances for the Church's Year

    Advent/Waiting
    Christmas/Celebration
    Epiphany/Mission
    Lent/Penitence
    Easter/Resurrection
    Ascensiontide/Heaven
    Pentecost/Holy Spirit

5   Homage and Blessing

6   Flags and Ribbons

7   Conclusion — Jive for Jesus?

1

Relaxation/Meditations

Relaxation.

'Be still and know that I am God' (Psalm 46:10).

Relaxation can be done at the start of a Christian dance class, especially if your group is tired after work, or just wants a time of meditation before the more energetic warm-up and exercise session. It can be done at the end of your evening, to lead you naturally into a time of open prayer before everyone goes home.

You need to feel safe and supported, warm and comfortable to begin. In a relaxed state, the body temperature tends to drop, and so it's important, if the relaxation comes at the end of your dance time, to put on a sweater or cover with a blanket, and definitely use a pair of socks! A foam or raffia mat is also useful if the floor is cold, or uncarpeted.

Music is optional. Some teachers use it after talking through the various stages of physical relaxation, and it can have a liberating effect. Disadvantages are that it can be divisive if someone isn't physically relaxed, and getting the choice of music just right is tricky.

Before you begin, it's good to give people permission *not* to participate if they really don't want to, and also to be aware that for some, lying prone is not easy or perhaps even possible. Suggest suitable alternative postures — eg sitting comfortably on a chair, with the back straight, and the feet on the floor, or lying on the tummy, with the head turned gently to one side. Remember that the object of the exercise is to make them feel comfortable, valued, and therefore more receptive to the Holy Spirit.

Whether you are leading this routine in a class, or using it in your own private devotions, it's a good idea to make a tape recording, then you can really enjoy it.

A simple technique to be read or memorised:

1. Make sure you are warm and comfortable, and have set aside this special time when you know you won't be disturbed.
2. Lie flat on your back on your mat — hands at the sides, palms up, a little way from the body. Feet about hip width apart. Close your eyes.
3. Begin with gentle breathing through the nostrils. Breathe out first, and let the in breath come in naturally. As you melt into the rhythm of this, you will feel any tension start to drain away.
4. Direct your thoughts to each part of the body in turn, to your muscles and joints. Think first about your left foot. Tense it and then relax it. Feel how heavy it is. Let your toes and foot and left ankle begin to feel completely relaxed. Now take your attention to your right foot — tense, relax, heavy — completely relaxed into the right ankle.
5. Now, think about your legs. Tense and relax them in turn up to and into the knee joints and above, into the heavy thigh muscles. Let your knees and thighs roll outwards, spreading into the mat.
6. Now, take your attention to your spine. Tense it as much as you can along the mat, feeling the elongation, then relax your whole back, feeling yourself sink into the mat.
7. Still breathing gently through your nose, draw your tummy muscles in against your spine, being aware of the tension you are creating. Then let the tension go, as your muscles go soft and loose.

8. Tense and then relax your upper chest. Your breathing is now slow and easy. Each time you breathe out, you relax a little more.

9. Think about your left hand. Tense and then relax your fingers so that they are limp and still. Now the fingers of your right hand. Let the relaxation spread up your arms as you tighten and then relax them. Tense your shoulders by shrugging them in turn and then let them lie back, completely relaxed.

10. Take your attention to your neck, where we often get very tight and tense. Lift your neck until you can feel the muscles tighten and then relax it. Each time you breathe out, relax your neck a little more.

11. Now, keep on breathing, slowly and steadily, through the nose. Mentally check your body, feet, legs, spine, tummy, hands and arms, neck and shoulders. If there is a part of you that is not relaxed, breathe relaxation into it, and let it go.

12. Think about your face. Screw up your features into a really tense grimace (don't worry, nobody but the Lord can see you!). Then, let the tension go. Smooth out your forehead, let your eyelids droop. Release the tension in your jaw, teeth slightly apart as your jaw relaxes and unwinds. Relax your tongue and throat.

13. Lastly, become aware of the all-over feeling of letting go into God's presence. Be aware of your breathing as his gift to you. Enjoy the feeling of mentally sunbathing in the glow of his love.

14. When it's time to end your relaxation session, it is important that you come back slowly. Wiggle your toes and hands a little. Gently stretch your arms over your head. Take your time as you open your eyes and become reaccustomed to your surroundings. Sit quietly for a while before you begin to move around again.

Meditations

In the Bible, we are encouraged to meditate regularly. In Psalm 1, for instance, we are told that the man who meditates on the law of the Lord 'day and night' is blessed. If meditating on God's law and his creation leads us into a closer union with him, then we are blessed indeed.

I have found the following simple meditations useful in deepening the atmosphere of prayer which leads naturally from a complete relaxation of body and mind. They could also be interpreted into 'movement prayers' if you or your group is led in that direction. Aids to meditation are left to your imagination, but music, flowers, paintings of beautiful places, all come to mind.

In India, meditation is known as 'tethering the drunken monkey' or 'stilling our invasive thoughts to get to the deep silence within', and the only way to really do that is to ask the Lord to slow us down. The following poem is taken from *The Treasury of the Holy Spirit* by Mgr Michael Buckley (p. 215).

SLOWING DOWN

Slow me down, Lord,
ease the pounding of my heart
by the quietening of my mind.
Teach me the art of slowing down,
to look at a flower,
to chat to a friend,
to read a few lines from a good book.
Remind me each day of the fable
of the hare and the tortoise
that I may know the race
is not always to the swift,
that there is more to life than
increasing its speed.
Let me look upward into the branches
of the towering oak,
and know that it grew great and strong
because it grew slowly and well.
Slow me down, Lord, and inspire
me to send my roots deep into
the soil of life's enduring values
that I may grow towards
the stars of my greater destiny. *Amen.*

A famous meditation from the Orthodox tradition is 'The Jesus Prayer', which simply asks: 'Lord Jesus Christ, Son of God, have mercy on me, a sinner.' It is possible to use this prayer in many ways in our everyday life in a practical and physical way by 'tuning' it to our breathing, heartbeat, and even walking:

Breathing:	*Out*:	'Lord Jesus Christ'
	In:	'Son of God'
	Out:	'Have mercy on me'
	In:	'A sinner.'

Heartbeat:	*1.*	'Lord Jesus'
	2.	'Christ'
	3.	'Son'
	4.	'Of God'
	5.	'Have mercy'
	6.	'On me'
	7.	'A sinner.'
	8.	Pause.

When walking:	*1st step:*	'Lord Jesus Christ'
	2nd step:	'Son of God'
	3rd step:	'Have mercy on me'
	4th step:	'A sinner.'

The famous holy man of peace, Mahatma Ghandi, is reputed to have once said to a Christian: 'A rose does not need to preach. It simply spreads its fragrance. Its fragrance is its sermon.' A simple but perfect meditation for a summer's evening, with perhaps a single lovely rose as a focal point.

Similarly, the famous seventeenth-century theologian, Thomas Traherne, speaks of the wonders of being one in perfect harmony with all our heavenly Father has made: 'You can never enjoy the world aright until the sea itself floweth in your veins till you are clothed with the heavens and crowned with the stars... till you can sing and rejoice and delight in God as misers do in gold and kings in sceptres, you never enjoy the world.' (From 'Centuries', 1.29.)

The final, modern meditation is my favourite, taken from the book *God's People on the Move* by Mary Jones and members of the Christian Dance Fellowship of Australia. It is written by Gillian Rubinstein:

THE CLOTH

He has spread out my life like a cloth
on the green grass under the sun.
It's attacked and eaten by moth,
torn, discoloured, undone.
Here are the wine stains of self
and the crumbs I gave everything for.
Oh Lord, put me back on the shelf!
Can't you see I'm no use any more?
With Love's bleach and Faith's laundry soap
He washes and rinses and airs,
and the sharp eyed needle of Hope
invisibly mends all the tears.
He has spread out my life like a cloth
Of linen, immaculate, fine,
and on it, in sign of his troth,
He has set out his bread, and his wine.

2
Warm-up/Exercises

Warm-up

Before you begin to dance, it's important that you 'warm up' muscles that might be tired or tense at the end of a day's work or study. Although the suggested movements are gentle and comparatively easy, it's also important that people should not strain or injure themselves. I therefore suggest that if you are leading a class, you should tactfully discover if anyone has any injury or serious illness, and suggest they seek medical advice before beginning any form of physical exercise. Class members should always be told that nothing you suggest is compulsory and that they can drop out or take a break whenever they feel the need during the course of the session.

A warm-up routine is also important in waking up the body and helping its owner become more aware of how it works, a bringing to consciousness of the parts we scarcely know we have, and a deepening awareness of God's Holy Spirit dwelling within.

STANDING STRETCH
1.	Stand with feet in parallel, tummy in, bottom in, breathing normally.
2.	Move your head around on your neck until it feels comfortable.
3.	Imagine a spring coming out of the top of your head, fixed to the ceiling, pulling you upright.
4.	With the pressure on the balls of your feet, gently bounce (if you have trouble balancing, try and fix your gaze on an unmoving point parallel with your eyes).

STRETCHING SPINE

1. Raise both arms towards ceiling. Look up, stretch first with the left, then with the right, fingers up. Stretch eight times slowly.

2. Drop quickly from the waist like a rag doll, towards the floor. Bounce gently in this position.

3. Uncurl from the base of your spine, one vertebra at a time, very slowly, until you are again in the standing position.

4. Repeat once.

WARMING UP SHOULDERS

1. Roll your right shoulder slowly backwards eight times. Repeat with left shoulder.

2. Roll your right shoulder slowly forwards eight times. Repeat with left shoulder.

RELAXING NECK

1. Gently tilt your head back on your neck, then forwards. Repeat.

2. Turn your head sideways to the left, then to the right. Repeat.

3. Roll your head on your neck downwards to the left, then to the right.

   (NB. Recent research suggests that rolling all the way round is not necessary and can cause undue strain.)

MOVING ARMS AND WAIST

1. Keeping the lower half of the body still, twist the upper half to the left while swinging both arms to the left with the hands at hip height, twist and swing back to the right.

2. Continue to twist to the left and then the right, each time swinging your arms to a higher point — waist, slightly above shoulders and finally up past your ears.

3. Continue to twist, this time swinging your arms a stage lower each time.

4. Repeat, with eyes closed.

LOOSENING LEGS
Legs are always pushed, never lifted up in dance. This allows for greater height and flexibility, and much less strain.

1. Stand with your feet in parallel position, and your weight on your left leg.

2. Push your right foot forward along the floor as far as it will comfortably go. Take it back in again.

3. Repeat this movement eight times.

4. Repeat with your left foot.

5. Push your right foot forward along the floor again until it is forced just into the air. Bring it back to the floor and take it back into position.

6. Repeat eight times.

7. Repeat with your left foot.

8. Push your right foot along the floor again, but continue to push until your foot is raised in front of you as high as you can manage. Bring it back to the floor at the point where it left and take it back into starting position.

9. Repeat eight times.

10. Repeat with your left foot.

To loosen the tension around your knees after this exercise, pull your knees up in turn to your chest, while standing.

Now sit down and bang your legs gently against the mat, one at a time and then together.

RELAXING FEET AND ANKLES
1. With legs stretched out, alternately point and flex your feet eight times. Try to keep heels off the floor.
2. Pull your knees up to your chest to release tension as before.

LOOSENING HIPS
1. While seated, put your feet together, soles facing; hold them in place with your hands around the toes; let your knees drop to the sides as far as they will go.
2. Keeping your tummy in, back straight and shoulders down, bounce your knees gently up and down.

RELAXING THE SPINE
1. Lie flat on floor, arms by your sides, palms downwards.
2. Place your feet on floor in parallel position, with bent knees, also in parallel.
3. Push down with your abdominal muscles to a count of four, trying to eliminate the space between your spine and the floor.
4. Relax to a count of four.
5. Repeat four times.

When you have finished, sit up slowly. Then stand up slowly.

Winding down

Just as warming up is important before dancing, so is winding down at the end of your session. This enables muscles to return to their more usual position, and indicates to your body and mind that this mode of working is now over. Winding down leads naturally into complete relaxation and prayer.

1. Stand as for the warm up, but with your feet slightly wider apart. Stretch upwards gently in your own time.

2. Let your arms drop to your sides.

3. Let your head drop on your neck. Bounce it gently.

4. Let your chest drop towards your waist. Bounce gently.

5. Let your body drop all the way over. Bounce gently.

6. Put your feet together. Uncurl slowly as for the warm-up, but this time allow the bones to settle back into place as you uncurl.

7. Breathe in slowly.

8. Breathe out slowly.

9. Breathe in slowly.

10. Breathe out slowly.

Exercises

1) Finding the centre

If we are to be truly graceful, and move with conviction, we need to move from our physical 'centre' — the part of the body from which all movement originates, or should ideally originate. Once we find this centre, it's also possible to become more aware of the spiritual and emotional core from which all of our being emanates — the still, small centre where we are most likely to experience the touch of God's hand, or hear the sound of his voice.

The following routine was first introduced to me by dancer Kate Jennings and has proved very helpful and illuminating.

1. Stand in parallel as for the warm-up. It may help to close your eyes.

2. Press one hand across the muscles of your lower back, just below the waist. Now swing your other arm and feel the muscles in your back moving.

3. Reduce the swing of your arm so that it is only one or two inches, and you will still feel your back muscles moving.

4. Now, still with one hand pressing your lower back, walk around in a small circle, swinging your free arm, and feel the complicated muscle dance that is going on in the centre of your lower back.

5. Then stand still and see if you can lift your free arm from that same point in your back. You will immediately feel that you are moving with a deep physical commitment, with understanding.

Experiment, moving other parts of your body, all from the centre. Once you begin to have a sense of always moving from there, it will become easier to control movement and be graceful. Think of yourself on a moving carousel. If you ran around the edge, you would have to run very fast just to keep up, but if you were at the centre, you could walk around its central pole slowly and with control.

2) Circling

1. Find a space well away from anyone else. Hold your arms out at shoulder height, palms facing downwards.

2. Start to turn, slowly at first, but getting faster and faster until you feel your hands taking your weight and leading your direction.

3. Try to slow down gradually.

(NB. It is best to try this with someone you trust, so that they can prevent you from banging into things and catch you if you fall!)

3) Exploring personal space

1. Begin by walking around the whole room for 8 counts (can be counted by drum beats, claps, or simply voices).

Stop walking and stretch out a part of your body for 4 counts. Hold it for 4 counts, then pull it in again for 4 counts. Repeat this 3 or 4 times. Use varying levels (high, middle, low) and different body parts each time.

2. Repeat the exercise, decreasing the amount of space to a half.

3. Then again halve the space and repeat the exercise.

The exercise concentrates on your body's movement through space, and the way it deals with other people's bodies appearing in that space. It is a very good, unthreatening way to encourage a new class to move around.

4) Moving in harmony

1. One member of the group takes up a pose in the middle of the room.

2. Another member is invited to take up a pose in relation to the first.

3. One by one, the members are invited to respond in this way until the whole group is arranged together.

4. The group then begins to move, each person responding to the others, the emphasis being on 'mutual caring' or 'harmony'.

5. As the movement takes over, appropriate music can be introduced.

5) Exercises in pairs

1. Get people into pairs. Encourage them to do 'mirroring' movements, taking it in turns to 'lead'.

2. Ask them to express, to each other, without words, what they have been doing that day, and/or how they are feeling.

3. Using Ecclesiastes 3 about time, get each pair to dance a certain phrase, eg 'A time to be born, and a time to die.'

6) Make up a dance

Making the transition from exercises to actual dancing need not be difficult if you bear in mind that simple dances can be devised using very basic movements. So once your group is warmed up and comfortable, try the following:

1. Raise hands slowly into the air above the head, and down again.
2. Join hands with group, move in and out.
3. Raise hands in the air as a group.
4. Circle to the right and left as a group.
5. All join hands in a line: step x number of steps to the right and left.
6. In fours, join right hands and move to the right; repeat, with left hands.

Do 'follow my leader', 'conga', 'circle into spiral' movements, and allow people to make up their own. Use a variety of music — pop, hymns, folk, classical — to change the mood. Take a simple, familiar chorus and create a dance, each person making suggestions. The beauty of this last idea is that, should you ever present it in church, the congregation will know it and provide an extra vocal accompaniment for your dance.

3

Simple Christian 'Signing' in Dance

Sign Language is a visual language formed by the hands, the arms, the body and the face, working together in a clearly co-ordinated manner. Though designed and developed for and by the deaf, 'signing' words or phrases within dance has become a vital part of the ministry of many members of the Christian Dance Fellowship.

There are, as you will see on the following pages, special 'church signs' which are invaluable to deaf and hearing alike in the interpretation of songs of praise and thanksgiving. Some churches have 'deaf choirs' and hold special services for people with hearing problems, and Lichfield is a diocese which supports this ministry through the diocesan council with deaf people, and chaplaincy work.

When using 'signing' in dance, it is important to remember that BSL or British Sign Language is a true language, the fourth most used indigenous language in the UK after English, Welsh and Gaelic. Gestures can have different meanings when performed at different heights, or with hand placements, so always be careful, and if you are in doubt about a particular 'sign' check on it, or leave it out.

A good, general rule is always to exaggerate the 'sign' using it as a basis for your own interpretation, but making it larger and more expressive than it would be in normal conversational signing. This way, those watching see that you are dancing as opposed to 'speaking' in sign language, but the meaning is not lost to anyone who cannot hear the music.

Useful hymns for dance 'signing'

As we are gathered, Jesus is here
Shine, Jesus, Shine
This is our God, the Servant King
Amazing Grace
How Great Thou Art
Holy, Holy, Holy

Church signs

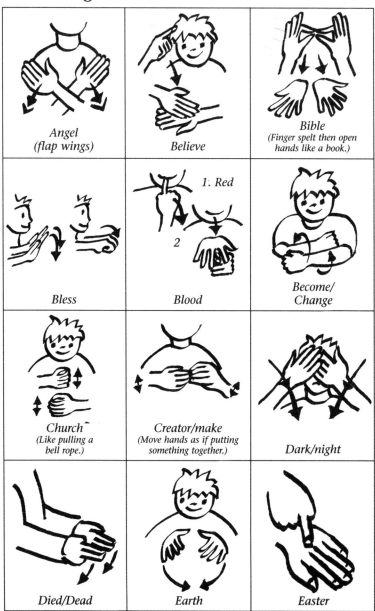

Angel
(flap wings)

Believe

Bible
(Finger spelt then open hands like a book.)

Bless

1: Red

2

Blood

Become/ Change

Church^
(Like pulling a bell rope.)

Creator/make
(Move hands as if putting something together.)

Dark/night

Died/Dead

Earth

Easter

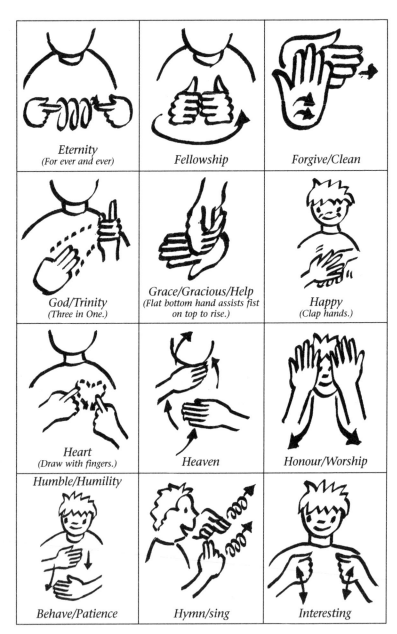

Eternity *(For ever and ever)*	**Fellowship**	**Forgive/Clean**
God/Trinity *(Three in One.)*	**Grace/Gracious/Help** *(Flat bottom hand assists fist on top to rise.)*	**Happy** *(Clap hands.)*
Heart *(Draw with fingers.)*	**Heaven**	**Honour/Worship**
Humble/Humility		
Behave/Patience	**Hymn/sing**	**Interesting**

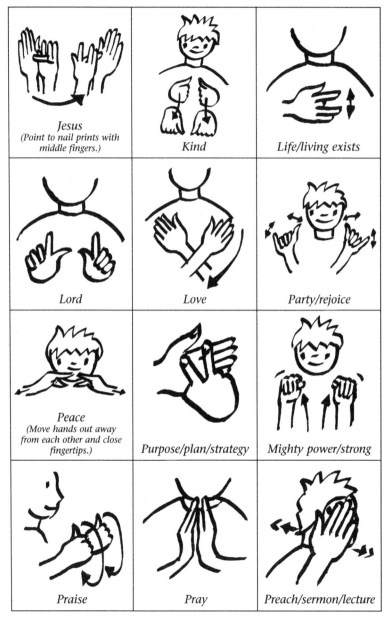

Jesus
(Point to nail prints with middle fingers.)

Kind

Life/living exists

Lord

Love

Party/rejoice

Peace
(Move hands out away from each other and close fingertips.)

Purpose/plan/strategy

Mighty power/strong

Praise

Pray

Preach/sermon/lecture

Worthy/precious	Real/true/sure	Rose/risen
Rule/reign (Move hands alternately forward and backward.)	Sacrifice	1. Save 2. Rich Salvation
Devil/Satan	Save	Sheep
Spirit/soul (Move hand away sideways and close fingers.)	Star	Story/explain/parable

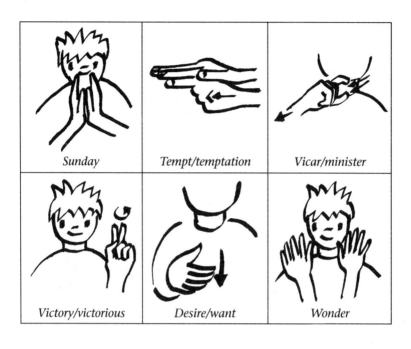

Sunday

Tempt/temptation

Vicar/minister

Victory/victorious

Desire/want

Wonder

4

Dances for the Church's Year

Advent/Waiting
Christmas/Celebration
Epiphany/Mission
Lent/Penitence
Easter/Resurrection
Ascensiontide/Heaven
Pentecost/Holy Spirit

Advent/Waiting

'Surely, I am coming soon! Amen!
Come, Lord Jesus!'
(Revelation 22:20).

From a Distance

Words and music: Julie Gold. Sung by Cliff Richard.
On 40th concert video and Event album, EMI TCCRTV31.

Timing: four minutes, 35 seconds (+five seconds).

A dance created for use in outreach, by Harvest Arts Group, first used on paved area (by Cavendish House) of Cheltenham Promenade, on Saturdays before Christmas, 1990. This version of the song has advantages for street work in that it has a good strong beat and musical arrangement, plus the familiar voice of Cliff Richard.
Numbers: 6–12.

1 2 3 4 5 6   Dancers begin in a line at the back of the
                 stage area, backs facing audience, feet
                 apart, arms down by sides.

From a distance
Alternate dancers half turn right to face
front, looking pose.

the world looks blue and green,
Rest of dancers half turn right to face
front, trace globe with hands in air (top to
bottom).

And the snow capped mountains so white. (2 beats.)
Make a mountain: Dancers at each end of line down on outside knee, arms diagonal 2nd, next bend both knees, next normal level, next on demi-pointe and/or lifting central person. (If no central person arms meet in a peak.)

From a distance the ocean meets the stream,
Central people face each other and, starting with arms high by inside shoulders, make large circle towards front, this is carried on by next pair, outer people take this ocean wave forward, crouching, arms opening out front, to make a stream.

And the eagle takes
All pose, feet together, arms 2nd curved elbows up, knees bent.

to flight. (2 beats.)
Flap arms up, straight knees, down, bend knees. Flap arms up, straight knees, down, bend knees.

****From a distance there is harmony,***
Run to circle, right arm in: 4th slight curve, side point left foot.

And it echoes through the land.*
In turn clockwise tip contents of arms into centre, hold new pose.

**It's the voice of hope,
One dancer runs front, arms and head uplifted.

It's the voice of peace,
Opposite number runs front, hands in dove shape.

It's the voice of everyone. (4 counts music.)**
Rest run to front, returning to previous formation, with gushing up movements from throat/mouth, with hands.

From a distance we all have enough, and no-one is in need.
Each dancer takes person on same line, sideways, as a partner. Alternate couples go to different sides, staggered across stage. Outers, ie 4, 2, 6, etc., sit, eating (scooping hands). The others mime offering food, which is refused.

There are no guns, no bombs, and no disease,
Seated dancers stand, one mimes firing a gun, another throws a grenade, the third enacts having a disease. Remainder hold hands and walk round clockwise in small circle, mid-stage right, facing in, oblivious to what happens around them.

No hungry mouths to feed.
Walkers continue, others freeze in pose.

For a moment we must be instruments, marching in a common band.
Marching to centre dancers make 2 lines, each mimes playing a different instrument as they continue to march to front stage, then peel off.

Playing songs of hope, playing songs of peace, they're the songs of everyone.
Repeat ** above.

God is watching us, God is watching us, God is watching us,
+Centre front stage crucifixion tableau is formed (Christ, two thieves). Just in front one dancer is the Virgin Mary, miming the laying of baby Jesus in a crib (two dancers crouch, arms crossed at wrists, to make manger). Others look on.+

From a distance.
All look up to the sky.

(Break 16 counts music, then 4.)
Starting with the person on outermost left side, dancers take each other by the hand and run round anti-clockwise, back to back, to make a circle.

From a distance you look like my friend,
Dancers face alternate directions to make a grand chain. (ie walk round offering facing person right hand, next person left hand, etc.) Pass two people by, pause at third ('friend'). Instead of shaking hands, turn back on them (half turn right).

Even though we are at war. (2 beats.)
Carry on chain in direction now faced, passing two people. On third instead of shaking hands, lunge forward, making a fist (same arm as leg).

From a distance I can't comprehend what all this war is for.
Hands either side of head, all walk in confused state, back to original starting positions, facing audience.

What we need is love and harmony, let it echo through the land,
Repeat * above.

It's the hope of hopes, it's the love of loves,
Repeat 'hope' as for ** above. For 'love' dancer hugs themself.

It's the heart of everyone,
Leaning forward, all move arms to 2nd,
then place over heart.

It's the hope of hopes, it's the love of loves, it's the song of everyone.
Repeat tableaux from + to + above.

(4 counts music.)
Drop positions, turn backs to audience, take four large steps back, into straight line. Half turn right to face front.

(Sing out) songs of hope, (sing out) songs of freedom, (sing out) songs of love, (sing out) songs of peace, (sing out) songs of justice, (sing out) songs of harmony, (sing out) songs of love.
Starting with 'hope' as for ** above, each dancer moves forward displaying a quality ('love', 'peace' and 'harmony' as before, for 'freedom' break imaginary wrist chains, for 'justice' raise fist of bent right arm in front, until arm is straight.)

(Sing out) everyone.
Make a circle facing in, hands on each other's shoulders.
[Note: 'Sing out' changes places now in the rhythm of things.]

(Sing out) sing songs of hope (sing out), sing songs of freedom (sing out), sing songs of love (sing out) sing songs of peace (sing out), sing out about justice (sing out), sing in harmony (sing out), sing about love (sing out).

Eight grapevine (Maim) left. (ie cross right foot over left, side step left on left foot, bring right crossed behind, side step left on left foot. Repeat all seven times.) NB done with speed – almost hopping in crossover parts.

Then change arm hold to basket (ie hold hands behind each other's backs). With right foot as an anchor in front, run round to right (now travelling in opposite direction), using left foot as pivot behind, leaning back.

Everyone (sing out).
Stop. Look up to sky leaning further back. Hold for five seconds after music ends.

Love Changes Everything

Words and music: Andrew Lloyd Webber/Don Black and Charles Hart, 'Love Changes Everything' sung by Michael Ball in *Aspects of Love*. Recorded on several albums including *All My Love* (Warner, esp. Polygram, 1997), 954835948-4
Choreography: Shirley Collins, spring 1998.

Timing: three minutes, twenty-three seconds.

This dance was choreographed for use in a Holy Communion service, in the round. It can be adapted, but requires a large space for ten to sixteen people. An even number is necessary. Dancers should have previous experience, and strong arm, leg and body lines. Fear, not hate, can be said to be the opposite of love ('Perfect love casts out fear' [1 John 4:18]). Dancers show different facial and bodily expressions to convey this to those who are watching.

As Scripture tells us to prefer one another in love, the floor patterns allow for pairs of dancers to each have a turn in full view. And there are some points where the dancers can improvise/dance prophetically. Though death is mentioned several times, air patterns are as bold as the music and reflect a sturdy form of joy. The logo of the Christian Dance Fellowship of Britain is incorporated.

```
< 1   1 >
  2   2
  3       3
4           4
5           5
  6       6
  7   7
    8 8
```

Introduction
Dancers are posed in a staggered height group, centre front, facing out. They can devise their own positions showing fear, cowering from each other and the world. Any male dancers are in 1, 2 and 3 positions.

Love, love changes everything, hands and faces

Starting with 1 on left side, in clockwise canon dancers straighten up, and with happy faces place hands just under chin — palms up, fingers splayed near cheeks, thumbs central.

earth

Dancers 5–8 throw arms out to side (palms up, thumbs outermost), in downward diagonals, indicating the earth beneath them.

and sky.

Rest of dancers throw arms out to sides (palms up, thumbs outermost), in upward diagonals, indicating the sky above them.

Love, love changes everything,

Bringing inner arm in front of body (folded gateway position), each dancer turns inward, putting this arm around or towards their opposite number (those lying have to twist from the waist up, legs still positioned on the floor).

how you live and

Palms facing down, dancers 1–6 throw arms up with energy, diagonally. 7s and 8s throw inner arm up, and grasp partner's outer arm at the elbow, straight in front, swivelling bodies to face each other, legs front, straight on floor.

how you die.
1–6 bring arms in front, palms together as if in prayer, as 7s and 8s gradually slide grip along partner's arm until they lie 'dead', flat on their backs.

Love/can make/the summer fly/or a/night/
1 / 2 / 3   / 4 / 5 /

seem like/a lifetime.
6 / 7 8

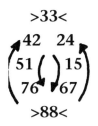

>33<

42 24

51( )15

76 67

>88<

The formation splits down the middle as dancers in pairs turn to face the back and take three large strides starting right foot, with an upward hop on the end, left foot pointed at knee (knees face front), arms 4th position (ie right arm up, left out to side). Solidus (/) above shows where each pair begins and how many times they do these steps. Travel is in a circular formation, and later pairs meet dancers coming the other way. 6s do a series out, then turn for a series back. 7s do not turn out, they stay facing each other and do a series, changing places. 8s merely stand and face each other.

*Yes love, love

Everyone should now have a partner facing them. The motif for love is to place the left arm, hand with little finger on chest and thumb up, over the heart, with the right hand palm up high above (slightly behind) the body, right foot pointed in front. However to get the arms into position, first throw left arm up in anti-clockwise circle, starting right arm off in similar direction on other side of body, as left arm reaches its highest point. (Right arm reaches its destination first.) Weight is on the left foot, body leans back slightly.

changes everything.*

Now all step forward on right foot, bringing arms down, palms almost touching partner's. Body leans forward, left hand slightly lower than right, left foot is pointed behind. Partners look lovingly at each other.

Now I tremble

Earlier were positions of fear. Now dancers show awe of God, knees slightly bent.

at your name.

Wherever dancers' arms are, they now bring hands together to right side of head, palms out, then pull left arm out to side, writing the name of God (in Hebrew one reads from right to left).

**Nothing
Dancers clap hands together and let
them spring apart.

in the world will ever**
Hand movement continues through arms,
which go outward in a circle as dancers
take a step right to turn back to back.

be the same.
Repeat from ** to ** above, turning back
to face each other. Then take a step
forward on outside leg, to be side by side.

Music count 1, 2, 3, 4.
Each couple poses in the CDFB logo, front
person making the vertical shape. The
positions are dropped on count '4' and
dancers take a step back again.

Love, love changes everything.
Repeat from * to *.

Days are longer
Grasp each other's hands in front and lean
back, arms and legs straight.

words mean more.
Free left hands and lean forward slightly
to touch partner's lips with fingers.

Love, love changes everything.
Repeat from * to *.

Pain is deeper than before.
Stomach contraction with arms, taking
one step forward on left foot, and turning.
Partners still face each other but now one
has back to centre, the other back to
audience.

***Love will turn your
Holding hands, arms are taken over the
head (to inside person's right side) and
dancers stand back to back, arms out at
sides, hands still held. Outside dancer
looses right hand and other dancer left
hand: they turn and face each other.

world around.***
Held hands are brought between bodies
and out the other side, as dancers take
two steps on inside legs, backs together
again. Arms are then taken back through
to other side, as feet remain still. (These
are ballroom/disco dance moves.)

And that world will last forever.
Repeat from *** to *** above.

Yes love, love changes everything.
Repeat from * to *.

Brings you glory, brings you shame.
Dancers 4, 1 and 5, centre back, make
crucifixion tableau. The rest kneel/crouch
in own positions, facing them.

Nothing in the world will ever
Dancer 1 in the tableau (ie 'Jesus') repeats
clapping movement **from 'Nothing' on
p. 97 (keeping feet still).

be the same.
Dancers 4 and 5 (ie 'the two thieves') repeat
clapping movement (keeping feet still).
Everyone else remains posed.

42
51
76
88
76
51
42
33

(Music)
Everyone runs clockwise to back left
corner, in pairs, to line up as shown on left
(3 3 are at front).

Off into the/world we go/planning futures/
3 3   /4 2   /5 1   /

shaping years./Love bursts in/and suddenly/
7 6   /8 8   /7 6   /

all our wisdom/disappears.
5 1   /4 2

Pairs come forward diagonally to front right
corner, as indicated by solidus above. Free
dance. They peel off alternately right, left,
then freeze.

Love makes fools of everyone,
The other dancer 1 (who was not 'Jesus')
jumps in the air and then embraces partner 5.

all the rules we make are broken.
8s run to 1s and 5s, all hug each other
(showing family love).

Yes love, love changes everyone,
Moves * on p. 96 are repeated, but 8s, 1s
and 5s do them in a circle, facing in, to
each other. Rest of dancers face the
audience.

live or perish in its flame.
All walk to centre, making flame
movements with arms.

***Love will never, never, let you be the
same. (Music.)***
Flames continue with slip steps right,
gaining speed. (Inner people almost on
spot, outer dancers take larger steps.)

***Love will never, never let you be the
same. (Music.)***
Turn and walk right, slowly and stately,
arms in 2nd position (out to sides at
shoulder level). In numerical order return
to start places, dancers facing in, inner
arm into centre, outer arm out, palms
facing down.

(Last note of music.)
All raise both arms inwards, joyfully,
palms up.

Christmas/Celebration

'The Word became flesh and made
his dwelling among us.
We have seen the glory of the One and Only,
who came from the Father,
full of grace and truth'
(John 1:14).

Silent Night

This simple walking dance is performed to the accompaniment of voices singing the first verse of the well-loved carol, and is most effective with lights off or dimmed. The 'spiral' is a very ancient form of dance whose origins are thought to go back to the fourth century.

Everyone stands in a circle. Candles are held by everyone in their left hands, their right hands placed on the shoulder of the person in front. Alternatively, just the first person (leader) and the last person can be given candles.

While singing the carol, all follow the leader, who moves from the circle into a spiral by walking, to the beat of the music, around the inside of the circle. Each person follows the person in front, starting to move when they feel a tug on their arm.

On reaching the centre of the spiral, the leader turns back on the line again and leads the dancers back into the original circle. People should be encouraged to look at each other as they pass.

A similar, very powerful walking dance for Easter is done with a circle of people, all holding hands, around a man-sized portable cross. As they walk, they sing the first verse of 'When I survey the wondrous cross', keeping their eyes on the cross as they match their footsteps to the beat of the music.

Come On and Celebrate

Words and music: Patricia Morgan, arranged by David Peacock.
Mission Praise, no. 99. Also other publications and recordings.
Choreography: Shirley Collins, 1986.

For dancers in congregations who want to move out. The
floor pattern is a free weaving between people. The air
pattern encourages others to participate, and is from a ballet
mime for happiness — which is to clap the hands together
while leaping up.

Begin by singing the whole song through once, dancers
seated or standing among the congregation. Second time
through dancers move as follows, singing throughout:

*Come on and celebrate! His gift of love
we will celebrate the Son of God, who
loved us and gave us life.*
Dancers walk out from the congregation
in all directions, clapping hands in time to
the music.

We'll shout Your praise, O King:
Continue walking, hands around mouth,
palms open and facing in.

You give us joy nothing else can bring;
Step and hop four times, alternate feet,
bringing bent arms down in front to waist
level, palms up.

we'll give to you our offering
Repeat steps and hops, lifting arms up
high.

in celebration praise.
Take a step to the side and turn until back
in same place.

*Come on and celebrate,
Eye-contact another dancer, run towards
them and clap hands twice, fast, after the
word *'celebrate'*.

celebrate,
Hold positions while singing, repeat fast
hand claps.

celebrate and sing,
Eye-contact and run to another dancer.

celebrate and sing to the King:*
Eye-contact and run to another dancer.

*Come on and celebrate, celebrate, cele-
brate and sing, celebrate and sing to the
King.*
Repeat from * to * above.

Epiphany/Mission

'Arise, shine, for your light has come,
and the glory of the Lord rises upon you.
Nations will come to your light, and kings to the
brightness of your dawn'
(Isaiah 60:1,3).

Shine Jesus Shine

Words and Music: Graham Kendrick. Widely published and recorded.
Choreography: Harvest Arts Group, notated by Shirley Collins.

Perhaps the best loved of all Kendrick songs, it allows everyone to give rip-roaring praise and worship to God.

Here the dancers use free moves during the verses, coming together as a group to present the chorus: easily copied by the congregation.

For the set part there is no floor pattern; for the free sections dancers cover the whole church — the aisles, at the back, choir, around baptismal and side chapel areas. The air pattern for each section involves strong, definite motions, high up and low down.

Three or more dancers are needed, in two straight lines with alternate placings. They occupy the available platform space at the front of the church, facing the congregation. Feet together, arms down.

Shine
Raise right arm straight, palm up.

Jesus Shine
Raise left arm up straight, palm up.

Fill this land with the Father's glory
Turning palms over bring arms down to waist level, wriggling fingers as if playing the piano. Front row keeps going down to kneel on one knee, side facing. (If a large group split, so some face either side.)

Blaze Spirit blaze
Bent arms in front of face, wave hands up and down to make 'flames'.

Set our/hearts/on/fire
Cross clenched fists over chest and tap four times, ie a beating heart.

Flow river flow
Step left on left foot, feet apart. At the same time bring bent right arm to right shoulder. Push right palm out diagonal left, bending left knee. Those who were kneeling stand to do this. All face front.

Flood the nations
Straighten knee so weight is on both feet, as right arm moves in front from left to right, palm down.

with grace and mercy
Carry on previous move to far right, turning palm up.

Send forth
Vertical right hand in front of face, thumb to nose.

your word,
Move arm away from face, straight down.

Lord
Raise right arm in front of body, palm in.

And let there
Begin to move arm down again.

be light.
Quickly raise arm, fingers splaying to make 'star'.

Light of the World
(John 1:4–5; 8:12; Matthew 5:14,16)

Words and music: D and I Butterfield, from *Sing Good News*
(Bible Society), a musical with songs using the Good News version of the Bible.
Choreography: Shirley Collins, 1982.

Timing: one minute, fifty seconds.

Light of the World

1. I am the light of the world.
   Whoever follows me will have the light of life.
   He will have the light of life,
   And will never walk in darkness,
   And will never walk in darkness

   > *Your light must shine,*
   > *your light must shine,*
   > *Your light must shine before people.*
   > *So they will see the good things you do*
   > *And praise your Father in heaven.*

2. The Word was the source of life,
   And this life brought light to mankind.
   The light shines in the darkness,
   And the darkness has never put it out,
   And the darkness has never put it out.

   (Repeat Chorus)

3. You are like light for the world.
   A city built on a hill cannot be hidden.
   Your light must shine so people
   Will see the good you do
   And praise your Father in heaven.

   (Repeat Chorus)

A praise piece in country dance style, for congregations in sets, or one group. Also fun for youngsters to present. An even number of people are required in batches of six or eight. Floor pattern makes an encircled star of David. Air pattern makes large and small flames, and swirls (inspired by the way fog behaves around street lights).

Begin with men and women on opposite sides in diagonal lines, facing each other.

I am the light of the world. Whoever follows me will have the light of life. He will have the light of life, And will never walk in darkness, And will never walk in darkness.
1 and 2 are partners. They hold palms together, curved as if sheltering a flame, and take twelve slip steps downstage on front leg, then skip backwards to end of line as next couple, 3 and 4, begin. Those waiting for a turn take a step towards the back on back leg as couples join end of line. Do this until everyone has a turn and is back in start position.

*(Chorus) Your light must shine, Your light must shine, Your light must shine before people,
1 and 2 skip to meet each other, join hands to change places, and go backwards into line. Other couples follow in succession.

So they will see the good things you do
All raise arms, palms out, and run foward. Pass partner by right shoulder, then fall back into line (passing left shoulder).

```
 _____
| 21      |
|      43 |
| 65      |
```

And praise your Father in heaven.*
1, 4 and 5 (ie alternate people on each side)
run forward to partners. All put right arm to
partner's left waist, raising left arm in air,
palm up. Run round in a circle together.

****The Word was the source of life,**
Partners loosen arms. They take right arm up
to side and overhead, to touch cupped
palms, then repeat with left.

And this life brought light to mankind.**
Each person cups own palms overhead,
skipping by partner's right shoulder and
back (past left shoulder).

**The light shines in the darkness, And the
darkness has never put it out,**
Repeat from ** to ** above.

```
 _____
 | 6   5 |
>| 4   3 |<
 | 2 1   |
```

And the darkness has never put it out.
Two hand turns: partners cross wrists and
join hands, skipping round and separating
into same formation as at the start, but at
opposite end.

*(Chorus) Your light must shine, Your light must
shine, Your light must shine before people, So
they will see the good things you do And praise
your Father in heaven.*
Repeat as for * to * above.

You are like light for the world. A city built on a hill cannot be hidden.
Run to centre and make a star: all put right hands in, left shoulders out, and go round clockwise.

Your light must shine so people
Walk backwards to make a circle, facing in, arms joined high.

Will see the good you do And praise your Father in heaven.
Grapevine to right: cross left foot over right in front, step to right on right foot (feet apart). Cross left foot over right behind, step to right on right foot (feet apart). Repeat all. Close feet together.

(Chorus) Your light must shine, Your light must shine, Your light must shine before people, So they will see the good things you do And praise your Father in heaven.
Repeat as for * to * above, but in the circle formation.

Lent/Penitence

'Create in me a pure heart,
O God,
and renew a steadfast spirit
within me'
(Psalm 51:11).

The Lord's Prayer

Words and music: Roger Jones, from *The Torn Curtain* (Christian Music Ministries, Birmingham, England).
Choreography: unknown source, scripted for this book by Shirley Collins.

As there is no floor pattern, and the air pattern uses high and lifted up movements, this dance could be done by two rows of people, standing on their chairs or pews at the sides of the church. As with many Christian dances, these movements are simple. What makes them special and effective is the inner conviction each dancer should have, inwardly praying the prayer and feeling emotion with the movements, not just waving their arms around.

Our Father in heaven
Right palm facing body, move arm in a circle from left to right, as if reaching to God, head up.

Hallowed be Your name
Left palm facing out, move arm up in a circle from right to left, as if shielding face from God's holiness. Head comes down with arm.

Your kingdom come
Raise right arm up straight, palm up, head following.

Your will be done
Repeat with left arm.

On earth
Make globe shape with hands in front of body from top to bottom.

As it is in heaven
Last movement should have ended palms up, fingers making a platform. Now lift this hand position above head (offering God the earth).

Give us today
Bring hands together side by side as if begging.

Our daily bread
Bring hands to mouth as if being fed.

Forgive us our sins
Cross arms wide over chest, head bowed, as if ashamed.

As we forgive
Push right arm out from left to right, palm up.
those who sin
Push left arm out from right to left, palm up.
against us
Lower both hands slightly and bow forward. Look around at congregation while doing these movements.

Instrumental — eight slow counts
Splaying fingers, bring hands together at
shoulder level, then lift arms (gathering
the people together and bringing them
before God).

Lead us not into temptation
Knees bent, lean back with bent arms
crossed above body, fists clenched, as if
fighting something off.

But deliver us from
Bring arms down, palms together as if
praying.

evil
Shoot arms out to sides quickly.

For the kingdom
Hold bent right arm in front of body,
palm out, and raise it in straight line over
head.

The power
Repeat with left arm.

And the glory are Yours
Wave arms to right, then left.

For ever and ever Amen
Bring arms down, palms together again, as if in prayer.

For ever and ever
Hold position, head bowed.

Amen.
Repeat shooting out of arms to sides.

We Being Many

Words and music: Mary Goetz, sung by Helen Shapiro and Cliff Richard on the album *Nothing but the Best (ICC)*. Scripture references: Romans 12:5; John 10:16.
Choreography: Shirley Collins.

Timing: four minutes, forty-three seconds.

This is a prayer of reconciliation and has been used for the bringing together of Jews and Christians, citizens of Northern Ireland and Eire, and the families of Windsor, Spencer and Al Fayed on the death of Diana, Princess of Wales. The formations for this dance can be adapted depending on the venue and situation. A symbol of Jesus on the cross is needed — preferably a male dancer — but it can be a simple wooden cross, statue, banner or painting. This needs to be lit where indicated, and can disappear into the background at other times.

LR LR LR

Dancers are arranged in six straight lines (L1 is first left line, etc), facing a partner. All are in a raised kneeling position (ie not sitting on the backs of the legs) with the knees facing slightly to the left, making diagonals. Arms are at sides. No one moves until the singer begins.

And we being many are
For a count of three, all raise right arm, palm out, head following.

one body
Repeat with left arm.

in Messiah
Lean back, then straighten, bringing arms down and turning palms in — you are accepting the Messiah into yourself.

And everyone
Turn arms upside down so elbows are uppermost.

members of
Stretch left arm forward and left leg, bent at knee.

one another
Stretch right arm back. Everyone should now be holding hands with the people in front and behind.

Loving each other.
Lunge forward and rest left cheek on your arm.

with God as our Father
Lean back, looking up to heaven, taking weight on back leg and straightening front leg.

Who loves us as a mother loves her
Straighten up and bend front leg again, to stand on it. Close with back foot. Keeping the flow of movement, let go of hands. R bring left and L bring right arms straight up and over head. As they do so, all R turn to face front.

new-born child
Each make a cradle with arms to hold a baby, the inner, raised arm, coming down to just below shoulder level, forming the highest part.

We are his
Cover face with hands, palms in.

bride,
Shoot hands up and out — look happy as you remove your bridal veil!

taken from his side
Bring arms in, hands to ribs on right side, push in and pull out movement. This signifies two things: Christ's bride coming from him, like Eve from Adam's rib, and the spear piercing Jesus on the cross.

When blood and water fell from the
Crucifixion position: turn feet slightly to left and bend knees, stretching out arms strongly. Head on left shoulder. Use your face to show his agony.

broken heart
Straighten up, feet still together. Make a heart with your hands, over your own heart. Thumbs make top side of a triangle.

of Israel
Show God's broken heart by jerking right arm down, and bringing left up. Hold positions.

The symbol of Jesus is lit at this point.

Count 1, 2,   / 3, 4
See the Lord provide / the precious Lamb
          / 5, 6
who died / The great 'I Am' who cried,
Starting with left foot, L3 and R3 walk diagonal back left slowly, six steps, left arm raised.
L2 and R2 wait two counts, then follow with four steps.
L1 and R1 wait four counts, then follow with two steps.

'Eli, Eli,
All take one more step on left foot, going into fourth position, and raising right arm. Everyone should now face the symbol of Jesus.

Lama Azavtani,
Lean forward and bow, arms coming down to floor and going behind back.

Abba, El Shaddai,
Reverse, coming up, arms high.

to God I give my life'
Large step back on right leg, turning on half pointe. Repeat step and turn, end facing partner. Go back to start position.

And we being many... new-born child
Repeat all from start to this point in dance.

(Instrumental break)
Hold partner round waist with right arm and walk round quickly clockwise in a circle twice, until back in place; looking each other straight in the eyes, arms out slightly. Change arm hold to left, and repeat in opposite direction.

Change arms so innermost are linked at the waist at the rear. R person lunges right on right leg, taking weight of L, who lifts outer leg and arm slowly to the side. Repeat in other direction, with L taking weight of R.

We are his bride... I give my life' Who loves us as a mother loves her new-born child.
Repeat as before, but do not go down to kneel at end. Instead, bend knees at end of turns, bringing feet together and arms down in front of body, then raise inner arm out, up and over, to go into cradle mime as before.

The light can go out on the symbol of Jesus.

(Fade)
Take partner's waist with right arm as before. Sway right to left for eight counts. One person is facing front, the other back. The six lines have become three.

Continue the movement but on the inward sway, take a step towards the centre. When the L2 and R2 couples are reached, left arms are grasped around their waist. Keep swaying until music ends. The effect is a large mass of people, moving together in unity.

Easter/Resurrection

'It is true!
The Lord has risen'
(Luke 24:34).

God Is Good

Words and music: Graham Kendrick (Kingsway's Thankyou Music, Eastbourne). 'God Is Good' appears on *Lights to the World* (Word UK Ltd, SOPC 2001).
Choreography: Shirley Collins. The choreography will fit other pieces of music with a similar rhythm to 'God Is Good'.

This is an Israeli praise dance, performed in circle formation. It is a dance for any number of people, and can be used by whole congregations or a church's dance group. It is suggested that the dance is performed four times.

This dance was first performed by the young people of St Brelade's churches, Jersey, during spring bank holiday 1989.

Begin after an introductory count of four beats.

God is good, we sing and shout it, God is good we celebrate,
Grapevine step four times to left: Begin by taking right foot over left, then step left on left so feet apart, then cross right foot behind left foot, then step left on left so feet apart. This is one whole grapevine. At end close feet together, thus missing last step.

God is good, no more we doubt it,
Step to right on right foot and kick left leg out in front (low kick). Repeat to left, and again to right. You should end with left leg in air: take it back in and stamp on it, then stamp on right leg — at the same time breaking handclasp to make two claps, one for each stamp.

God is good, we know it's true.
Repeat step and kick sequence as above, starting on left leg. You should end with right leg in the air: take it back and out to the right side, step on it and execute a full turn, raising arms high.

And when I think of his love for me, My heart fills with praise, And I feel like dancing, For in his heart there is room for me, And I run with arms open wide.
(You should have ended facing the centre again, feet together.) Join hands again and repeat the whole dance.

(Last time)
Bring arms down at end of turn, to raise again in front, at the same time executing a small jump, feet together, from and to a plié (bent knee position). Shout 'Hey!' as you jump and look up.

(Finish)
By straightening knees. Hold position for a few seconds.

Hosanna!

Words and music: John Wimber.

Formation: large circle, in twos, facing partner. A face clockwise. B face anti-clockwise.

Hosanna, hosanna
Chain — give R hand to partner, L hand to next person and so on round circle for eight skips.

Hosanna in the highest
Three skips towards next partner, hop and clap high.
Three skips backwards and hop, clap low behind back.

Hosanna, hosanna, hosanna in the highest
Repeat all of above.

Lord we lift up your name
As turn inwards on spot, raise arms.

with hearts full of praise
Bs turn outwards on spot, raise arms.

Be exalted O Lord my God
Bow low and 'scoop' up praises, and 'throw' the praises up high.

Hosanna in the highest
Turn back to starting positions, waving imaginary banner as you do so, and then lower arms ready to start again with chain.

Glory, glory, etc.
Repeat all of above.

(Instrumental for eight counts)
Step together on spot — 'move' with the rhythm.

Hosanna, hosanna, etc.
Either repeat as before, *or* all face centre and hold hands, slipping steps to left in place of eight skips, step hops/claps to centre.

Hosanna, hosanna, etc. (percussion only)
Step together, clap to each side.

Lord we lift up your name, etc.
Movements as before.

Lord we lift up your name (etc. to end)
Movements as before.

Be exalted O Lord (to end).
Move towards centre, raising hands. All hands raised, either still, or 'waving' as if sea of praise.

Ascensiontide/Heaven

'Salvation belongs to our God,
who sits on the throne,
and to the Lamb'
(Revelation 7:10).

All Heaven Declares

Words and music: Noel and Tricia Richards (Kingsway's Thankyou Music, Eastbourne). This version is by John Perry, recorded on his album *All Heaven Declares* (Kingsway SFC 197). *Mission Praise*, no. 14. **Choreography:** young children of St Brelade's churches, Jersey.

Timing: two minutes, twenty-five seconds.

A simple worship dance for any number of people, in a circle formation. Floor and air patterns show humility before God, with adoration of the risen Jesus.

```
        v
  >   O   <
        ^
```
Begin facing in, kneeling with backs of legs touching feet. Fingertips are just touching the floor, palms facing out.

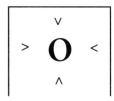

All heaven declares
Bring hands together, as if praying.

the glory of the risen Lord.
Part palms from thumbs, as if opening a book to read (the Bible).

Who can compare with the beauty of the Lord?
Hands the same, raise arms (offering the Bible to God). Loose hands and lower arms while standing.

Forever he will be the lamb upon the throne.
Walk round to right in a circle very slowly, raising arms and reaching up (trying to touch Jesus on the throne).

*I gladly bow the knee and worship him alone.**
Bow down on left knee, bending forward, taking arms back slowly. Then lower right knee, bringing arms forward, to end as you began.

I will proclaim the glory of the risen Lord. Who once was slain to reconcile man to God. Forever you will be the lamb upon the throne. I gladly bow the knee and worship you alone.
Following the music again, repeat all, but end crouching so you can stand quickly to repeat movements to the last lines of the song from * to * above.

To end, keep left knee only on the floor, sit on it and stretch right leg out in front as arms come forward. Front of body rests on extended leg.

Hold final position until music has completely faded away.

I am with you always (Matthew 28:20).

Words and music: Paul McCartney, 'Celebration' the final part of
Standing Stone, London Symphony Orchestra conducted by
Lawrence Foster (EMI 1997, 7243 5 56484 4 0).
Choreography: Shirley Collins, May 1998.

Timing: three minutes, fifty seconds.

C		
1∣		∣5
2∣	X	∣6
3∣		∣7
4∣		∣8

This dance follows the story of Christ
from Easter Sunday to Ascension Day. It
works best with a large number of people
— around forty. Only eight need previous
experience in movement. The emotions of
those taking part, and the congregation,
are likely to be stirred. As the disciples
searched for Jesus, and later watched him ascend to heaven,
his love was reaching out to them. It is still reaching out.

As well as being suitable for the stage, this dance is also
effective when presented in a large open space, eg outdoors,
a church hall, or church with seating moved away. Air
pattern: a huge crowd moves in an apparently natural way.
This is achieved by use of alternate limbs in the ordered
lines, and each dancer's personal choice to lunge standing or
kneeling at the end. Floor pattern: running round in a circle,
as we tend to do in life, becomes an ordered pattern as we
are drawn to Jesus Christ, within which we can each move
in our own way.

As the music begins, people are crowded off stage to
sides, in four lines to either side (around four to a line). X
on the diagram above marks the spot where white grave
clothes have been left (concealing wording for the end). C at
the back is a chair, ladder or raised area. Numbers 1–8 show
the lines of people.

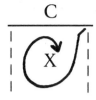

C

Main theme with singers: 16 fast counts

Eight experienced dancers enter back stage left, also in a line, moving to right in clockwise circle around the grave clothes, walking mournfully — sixteen steps starting with right foot.

2 fast counts

They pause momentarily, realising the tomb is empty (facial expression, surprise).

6 fast counts

They quicken their pace, run round and out to sides, each facing a line of people.

```
          C
 1|1          5|5
 2|2    X     6|6
 3|3          7|7
 4|4          8|8
```

2 slow counts

Diagram numbers in bold type show the more experienced dancers. They beckon with the right arm, then the left. (Facial expression great joy, ie 'Come and see, he has risen!')

```
          C
 111          555
 222    X     666
 333          777
 444          888
```

Main theme repeated: 16 slow counts

Now travelling much slower (ie funeral-march speed) with raised foot closing behind with pointed foot, and bent knee, arms down: eight lines take sixteen steps forward — first person begins with right foot, second with left, third with right, etc. Experienced eight take sixteen steps backwards starting with right foot, arms out in front at shoulder level, palms up. Then eight experienced (who should have ended with right foot raised) step on right foot and half turn right, putting left behind, lowering arms. Everyone else stays still. Experienced eight are now fronting the eight lines.

2 slow counts

All contract at the stomach, bringing hands in, palms facing body. Then take one step forward bringing back foot through to step on it, arms going down, behind, up and over. (Facial expression and body language: grief at Jesus' death.)

2 slow counts

Repeat from * to * above.
Hold last position momentarily as singers/ music pause.

4 slow counts

Repeat from * to * above, twice.

Main theme repeats: 20 slow counts

Now everyone brings raised back foot forward (to stand feet apart), rocking to side on it, the first of twelve rocks to alternate sides (front eight start to left), arms rising in front to shoulder level, palms up. (Facial expression: wonder, 'He is risen!') Then bend arms and bring in to chest, fists clenched (gleeful excitement), carry on rocking with shoulders only turning four times (front eight start to left). Finally, throw arms out to sides alternately four times (front eight start to left), palms up, looking at nearest person (swing arms in front to get to other side).

Music climbs in four sweeps

Eight front dancers rush forward immediately. (Designated one, concealed by other dancers, picks up grave clothes, opens up message 'I am with you always', and fixes it on extending pole.) The rest run forward on third and fourth sweeps so all face back of stage (some are side angled).

Musical climax

Designated dancer holds up text on pole, covering self apart from feet (they are not meant to portray Jesus, the text does). As the music reaches its climax the designated dancer walks slowly backwards and climbs onto raised area, then extends pole as high as it will go to signify the ascension. As this happens the rest lunge forward on one leg, arms outstretched in front. Each can decide whether they wish to do this standing or kneeling. (Facial expression and body language, 'Don't go.')

Music and vocals trail away: 26 slow counts

As the text was shown, small pieces of paper (hidden in pocket at bottom of banner, released by person holding it) were scattered on the floor. In the order they feel led, dancers now reach to pick one up, and read it. Some will be facing audience, some not. (The papers can be any shape, ie hearts, doves or just plain slips. On each is written: 'I am with you always — Jesus (Matthew 28:20).'
Some wander off stage quickly, others linger.

Cut the scene either by fading light on the text, or lowering it reverently when everyone has received a paper slip. (In a proper theatre the banner could even be lifted up and literally ascend out of view.) Members of the audience to be offered a slip too, either by dancers bearing baskets in the auditorium, or by a pre-announcement to come on stage and pick one up.

Pentecost/Holy Spirit

'When you send your Spirit,
they are created,
and you renew
the face of the earth'
(Psalm 104:31).

The Feast of Pentecost

Music: *Zion* by Nigel Wright (available from Shirley Collins) –
originally written for a CMJ/CDFB musical, *Jigsaw* where it showed
the new Jerusalem being built from dry bones/mourning people.
Choreography: Shirley Collins.

Timing: six minutes, fifty seconds.

Modern dance for 16–30 people. First performed by Catholic
teenagers for the Diocese of Clifton's youth liturgy, July 1998.

Dancers are in 3 groups plus 1 spiritually
experienced person to play the Holy Spirit.
As the piece begins group 1 are in a line
centre stage facing left, feet apart. They
are a wall. Arms rest on next person's,
those at either end have outer arm down,
arms of central pair touch at fingers only.

Mournful music – 16 slow counts
Group 2, beggars, the lame and infirm
drag themselves on from back stage left to
crouch/sit stage right, facing left.

Mournful music builds – 8 counts
Ignoring group 2 who reach out, a disciple
walks on from back stage right, to mime
unlocking a door in centre of wall. Inner
arms of central pair in wall are pushed
forward by disciple – a stable door
opening.
Mournful music builds – 8 counts
Also ignoring group 2 more disciples
wander on from back stage right and left.
They go through swinging door = group 3,
circle facing in.

Single drum beats: 1 / 2
Disciples kneel / pray hands together
/ 3
/ bow heads

Mysterious music
Holy Spirit enters back stage left, trailing large piece of white material. Runs around outside of group 3 circle twice before entering, to drape cloth over each person in turn: actually praying over them.
Drum rolls
Holy Spirit wafts cloth up and down quickly. Then exits back stage left.

Keyboard beat – 16 counts
Disciples waft hands up and down in front of body – tongues of fire.
Keyboard beat – 48 counts
In slow motion they stand (stop waving arms), walk right in own circle. When all back facing centre lift arms up and over head to rest on shoulders of people to right and left (still slow motion), feet together. Then sway shoulders left, right.

Cymbal beats
Stop swaying on first beat, bend knees on second. Then begin grapevine x 10 to right, starting with a step right (cut last step, end feet together). Group 2 draw near to peer under door and through cracks in wall.
Main theme quiet
Groups 1 and 3 grapevines x 6 left, group 1 make line at back, facing front. They ended right foot in front and now pivot

right on it, to space out and make 3 lines, facing front.

Main theme louder

Groups 1 and 3 hitchhiker R, L, RR, x 8 (alternate arms).

Jump to 2nd position of feet, arms bent at sides, and in, right leg bent at knee x 8 (alternate legs). Pivot turn x 2 right, end facing stage right.

Feet apart, arms out straight at front shoulder level, 1st fingers pointed at group 2, sway, starting right x 8.

Main theme very loud

Groups 1 and 3 march on spot x 8, causing Group 2 to shuffle back stage right, in fear. Groups 1 and 3 march forward x 8.

Climax begins

In pairs, groups 1 and 3 go to a poor person and pose, hands splayed above them. Healings take place, they rise, limbs grow! (Some arms and legs previously hidden.)

Climax proper

Much free leaping about.

Fading away.

Dancers come off stage area down through congregation to exit.

Peace Like a River

Words and music: Dave Markee, Chris Roe, Kingsway's Thankyou Music, Eastbourne.
Choreography: Damien, Liz , Jean and Rowena.
Illustations: Rowena Webb.

As the music begins the dancers are standing in a circle facing in a clockwise direction. On the fifth bar alternate dancers move clockwise with their arms curved before them as though carrying an armful of blessings to the next person. As the sixth bar begins the next people receive the blessings and move on round, etc, until the introduction finishes. If there is a focal point (such as a cross), the arms could be raised here to receive from the Lord and the arms lowered, reaching out from the circle on the opposite side as though sharing the blessing with the world.

Peace like a river
On the word *'Peace'*, everyone sweeps towards a focal point together and stands with their arms reaching up, hands together as in

prayer.

'... like a river'.

All dancers turn to face each other in two groups and move a few sideways steps swiftly away from the focal point, lowering their arms and swinging them across their bodies to finish standing still with their arms outstretched on the end of the word *'river'*.

Love like a mountain

The dancers sweep back to the focal point together, crossing their arms over the chest (*'love'*), facing each other as two groups and lift the arm nearer the cross to full diagonal stretch while the other arm is lowered to complete the line. Look up along the higher arm.

The wind of your Spirit is blowing everywhere

All dancers spread out, moving and turning freely with generous arm movements to express the blowing of the wind.

Joy like a fountain

Dancers step forward on right foot to form a circle all facing inwards. As the step forward is taken, the left foot is pointed and raised to the side slightly while the arms burst upwards and outwards to express joy. Continue to move in a couple of steps with all hands reaching down and forwards into a central cluster. On the word *'fountain'*, raise all hands straight up then walk backwards as the arms move outwards and down with the fingers moving in a sprinkling action.

Healing spring of life

On the words *'Healing spring'*, dancers move clockwise while drawing close enough to form a circle joined by their right hand resting upon the right shoulder of the person in front. While continuing to walk round clockwise, bring the left arm over from behind and rest the left hand on top of the right hand on the other person's shoulder (*'… of life'*).

Come, Holy Spirit

Dancers look up above the centre of their circle and raise the right arm as they begin to move away from each other.

Let your fire fall

Dancers move into their own space to move individually.

Repeat. Regroup to begin the verse again. Any musical breaks can be used for free movement.

5

Homage and Blessing

A Creed in movement

We believe (Arm raised above head, with feet apart.)

that God sent his Son Jesus into the world. (Hands brought down close together and stretched out in front of body.)

He became man through the Holy Spirit (Hands crossed to symbolise the wings of a dove.)

He was born of the Virgin Mary. (Hands clasped in a mime of cradling by a mother, with head down and eyes cast down.)

He was crucified (Arms stretched out.)

died (Head dropped forward.)

and was buried (Head on arm.)

He went down to those below (Fingers touching ground.)

Afterwards, he rose from the dead (Arms raised, stretched in front of body, parallel to ground, palms up.)

And he went up into heaven to exist at God's right hand (Hands raised above head.)

There he prays for us always (Palms of hands together above the head.)

Praise the Lord! (Hands outspread above the head.)

God lives in me (*Sarum Prima*)

God be in my head	(Touch head.)
And in my understanding.	(Lift hands upwards.)
God be in my eyes	(Touch eyes.)
And in my looking	(Point hands outwards.)
God be in my mouth	(Touch mouth.)
And in my speaking.	(Drop hands downwards.)
God be in my heart	(Touch chest.)
And in my thinking.	(Cross arms across chest.)
God be at my end	(Hands by sides.)
And in my departing.	(Bow head.)

Kenyan blessing

Taken from *A Kenyan Service of Holy Communion* (Church of the Province of Kenya, 1989).

The people accompany their first three responses with a sweep of the arm towards the cross behind the altar, and their final response with a sweep towards heaven.

Leader:	*All our problems*
People:	*We send to the cross of Christ.*
Leader:	*All our difficulties*
People:	*We send to the cross of Christ.*
Leader:	*All the devil's works*
People:	*We send to the cross of Christ.*
Minister:	*All our hopes*
People:	*We set on the risen Christ.*

6

Flags and Ribbons

Dancing with flags and ribbons is becoming increasingly popular in some churches, and also at events such as Spring Harvest. The attraction is easy to see and hear, for a brightly coloured flag not only makes a visual impact, it creates a wonderful, satisfying 'swishing' sound as it slices through the air, bringing to mind the season of Pentecost, and the rushing wind of the Holy Spirit.

With simple movements such as a sideways figure eight, a wave or a circle, it is possible to create a very dramatic effect, particularly if different coloured flags are used, interspersed with long satin ribbons on sticks.

According to Marie Bensley, author of *Moving in Praise with Flags* (p. 20), the colours of flags can represent:

Gold for kingship, majesty, glory of heaven.

Silver for God's gifts, as in the Holy Spirit.

Red for salvation, the blood of Christ, and sacrifice.

Blue for heaven, water or splendour.

White for holiness, purity and cleansing.

Purple for kingship, majesty, 'the purple robe', grace.

Orange for fire, power, also the Holy Spirit.

Yellow for light, joy and celebration.

Green for creation, new life and healing.

Black for death and sin.

Another advantage of flags and ribbons is that they can be used in the aisles of churches in procession; movement can be spontaneous and congregation members be encouraged to join in. Most people seem to be attracted, and are eager to 'have a go' even if only once, with a brightly coloured accessory which adds height and flair to their initially tentative movements.

Flags and ribbons can be used to illustrate a Bible story, or to give a hymn or chorus that added visual effect which brings it truly to life.

Why not try the song, 'The Battle Belongs to the Lord', with two 'camps' (darkness and light) acting out the words with flags and ribbons flying and falling, threatening and retreating, with a final victory coming with the flying of the golden flag of the kingship of Jesus?

A final word of warning. Do be careful when using flags and ribbons. Make sure there is space, and no one is in danger of being hit. Never wave flags while standing in the congregation and always check with the church leadership before you begin. It's also important that children (who always insist on choosing the biggest flags!) are well supervised.

How to make your own flag

Materials needed:

Lightweight fabric, approximately 1.5 m by 1.1 m.
dowelling or bamboo stick 12 mm by 1.5 m. 4 'sticky fixers' (available from good hardware counters).
loads of patience!

1. Neaten edges of material where appropriate to prevent fraying.

2. On one of the 1.1 m sides, sew a hem or tubing of approximately 5 cms.

3. Feed the dowelling through the tubing until the two ends are exposed.

4. Place two 'sticky fixers' at one end of the dowelling, pull fabric over these and press firmly, making sure that the top edge of the fabric is level with the top of the pole.

5. Pull fabric down pole until taut to find where to put the bottom two 'sticky fixers'. Move fabric up the pole slightly while putting fixers in place. Pull fabric back over fixers and press firmly.

6. Your flags should now be ready to use, but make sure the end of the pole is smooth to avoid splinters.

(Directions from Val Whiley.)

Ready-made flags can be purchased from:

Movement in Worship
c/o City Gate Church
84–86 London Road
Brighton
BN1 4JF.

Ribbon and wand assembly instructions

Materials needed:

Dowelling approximately 27 cms long, 3 cms in diameter.
Ribbon 3.5 cms wide by 5 m long.

Split ring 2 cms in diameter.

Chain as illustrated, shortened to approximately 7 cms.

(A sink plug bought from hardware shop has ideal chain and connections.)

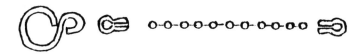

Assembly:

Take length of dowelling and round off one end.
Attach shortened chain into flat end of wand with screw through chain connector.

Insert approximately 3 cms of ribbon through split ring and sew to other side neatly.

Dip the other end of ribbon into melted candle wax to prevent fraying.

Attach split ring to chain.

For a different effect, use four lengths of ribbon approximately 130 cms long attached together through ring.

(Directions from Val Whiley.)

Crêpe paper ribbon/streamer

Materials needed:

'Spring' wooden or plastic clothes pegs.

Length of twine, approximately 15 cms long for each streamer.

Packets of crêpe paper, various colours, cut into ribbon strips 4 cms wide.

Method:

Thread twine through metal fastening on peg. Tie firmly to make short 'string'. Open peg and clip two lengths of contrasting crêpe paper ribbon into the 'mouth'.

Use string to 'fly' paper streamer in patterns of colour to illustrate your dances. This is very effective with youngsters, who also enjoy making them.

(Directions from Kathryn Slater.)

Ready-made ribbons and wands are available from:

Carita House
Designer Leisurewear
Stapeley
Nantwich
Cheshire
CW5 7LJ.

Portable cross in three parts

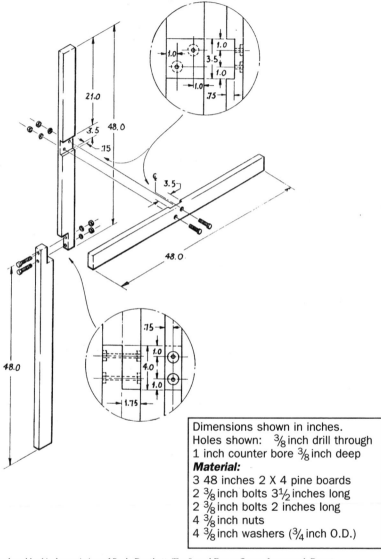

Dimensions shown in inches.
Holes shown: ³⁄₈ inch drill through
1 inch counter bore ³⁄₈ inch deep
Material:
3 48 inches 2 X 4 pine boards
2 ³⁄₈ inch bolts 3¹⁄₂ inches long
2 ³⁄₈ inch bolts 2 inches long
4 ³⁄₈ inch nuts
4 ³⁄₈ inch washers (³⁄₄ inch O.D.)

Reproduced by kind permission of Paula Douthett. The Sacred Dance Group, Longmead, Dorset.

Conclusion
— *Jive for Jesus?*

'I really love this song!' my new friend, Annie Stones, exclaimed as she began to move to the Christian dance music we were playing together in St Chad's church hall.

Exactly the same age, Annie and I had discovered we had many other things in common. We had lived through the penny-pinching fifties and the swinging sixties, and brought up our children in the seventies.

Both converts, we had found Jesus Christ as adults, and had our lives transformed, she being led to full involvement in the Baptist church, me coming to ordination and parish ministry. Apart from all that, I had been drawn to Annie immediately by her vitality — a liveliness that spilled out of her eyes and lit up her face in a smile that was both warm and engaging.

Like me, she loved to dance, having led a worship group at her Wolverhampton church until her friend and dance partner left, her husband's work taking them to another town. Although we had never danced together, hardly, in fact, knew each other, I sensed Annie would not be inhibited by our bare and rather dusty hall, echoing incongruously with lively praise music on a rainy Friday afternoon.

The beauty of dance, as I keep on discovering, is that the Lord can and does use it to draw us closer to each other and to him. Through the power of the Holy Spirit, he encourages us so much that worship is irresistible.

And so, as the music changed to a more up-beat song about Jesus, Annie and I both moved more rhythmically, eating up the inches of floor, moving our hands and arms in union with our lightly tripping feet. Dancing separately, and yet, almost without realising it, dancing the same, suddenly familiar steps!

'Hey!' Suddenly I stopped dead, my memory twirling back across nearly four decades to a time I could scarcely remember, and the steps I would never forget. 'Did you ever' I grinned, 'go out and do the rock and roll?'

Annie blinked, and then grinned back. 'Did I ever?' she repeated, rhetorically. 'I never really stopped, when I was in my last year at school. Only we called it "bop".'

'And we had the underskirts, and the flat shoes.'

'And danced all night in praise of Elvis.'

It was fun reminiscing, but there was, I already knew, more to our conversation than that. As Annie and I began experimenting with the movements of the 'jive', we discovered that, like riding a bicycle or swimming, the art couldn't be forgotten.

'There must be lots of church people of our age who can dance like this,' I panted as I whirled round and under Annie's arm, 'who'd perhaps like to try Christian dance but don't think it's down to earth enough, and so are put off.'

'Look at how popular line dancing is,' my partner pointed out, leading me into another turn in time to the music. 'Lots of people in my church do that nowadays.'

'And tap and ballet. There's adult classes in both advertised now at the community centre!' I didn't add that only the pressures of parish ministry had stopped me from joining them, but I think Annie knew anyway.

'I think the Holy Spirit is saying we should use every skill to worship, whether people would find it strange or not,' she said as we later sat down for a time of prayer. 'After all, it says in the Scriptures, "with my whole heart, I will rejoice," and some of the modern Christian music has a definite country, or rock beat.'

'Jive for Jesus!' It had a certain ring to it that caught my imagination. Yet another dimension to all I had learnt since my first tentative movements at theological college.

And why should we stop there? Classical ballet is beautiful, and could be used imaginatively in churches just as contemporary dance is in musicals like *Jesus Christ, Superstar*.

To worship God, and find joy and healing in his dance, there should be no restriction. For surely the unseen arms we run into are eternal, and the circles we make indicative of our need to express, in our modern way, a very old sentiment. In the words of the American Shaker revival song 'Simple Gifts':

'Tis the gift to be simple,
'tis the gift to be free,
'tis the gift to come down where we ought to be.
And when we find ourselves in the place just right,
'Twill be in the valley of love and delight,
When true simplicity is gained,
To bow and to bend we shan't be ashamed.
To turn, turn will be our delight,
Till by turning, turning, we come round right.*

---

* Edward D. Andrews, *The People Called Shakers* (OUP: Oxford, 1953), p. 173.

APPENDIX
References to Dance in the Bible

Exodus 15:20	Israel's deliverance from the Red Sea
Exodus 32:19	Worship of the golden calf
Judges 11:34	Jephthah's return
Judges 21:21	Women of Shiloh
1 Samuel 18:6	David's victorious return
1 Samuel 21:11	David's praise sung in music and dance
1 Samuel 29:5	David's victorious return
2 Samuel 6:14	David dances before the ark
1 Kings 18:26	Worship of Baal
Job 21:11	Children singing and dancing
Psalm 30:11	Weeping and wailing/dancing and rejoicing
Psalm 149:3	Praise him in the dance
Psalm 150:4	Praise him in the dance
Ecclesiastes 3:4	Time to dance
Song of Songs 6:13	Wedding dance
Jeremiah 31:4	Joyful dance
Jeremiah 31:13	Maidens will dance and be glad
Lamentations 5:15	Dancing turned to mourning
Matthew 11:17	We played the flute for you
Matthew 14:6	Daughter of Herodias' dance
Mark 6:22	Daughter of Herodias' dance
Luke 7:32	We played the flute for you
Luke 15:25	We heard music — the prodigal son

Bibliography

Andrews, Edward D., *The People Called Shakers: A search for the perfect society* (OUP: Oxford, 1953).

Berry, Madeleine, *Know How To Use Dance In Worship* (Scripture Union: London, 1985).

Blogg, Martin, *Dance and the Christian Faith* (Hodder and Stoughton: London, 1985).

Buckley, Mgr Michael, Tony Castle, ed., *The Treasury of the Holy Spirit* (Hodder and Stoughton: London, 1984).

Church of the Province of Kenya: A Kenyan Service of Holy Communion (Uzima Press: Nairobi, 1989).

Davies, J.D., *Liturgical Dance* (SCM Press Ltd: London, 1984).

Jones, Mary, and members of the Christian Dance Fellowship of Australia, *God's People On the Move* (CDFA Press, 1988).

Long, Anne, *Praise Him In the Dance* (Hodder and Stoughton: London, 1976).

Raine, Andy, *I Will Be With You*, details from the author: 3, Lilburn Terrace, Holy Island, Northumberland.

Snowber Schroeder, Celeste, *Pray with Hearts and Hands* (Marshall Pickering, 1995).

Traherne, Thomas (Mowbray, 1975).

Useful Addresses

Christian Dance Fellowship of Britain, 25 Scardale Crescent, Scarborough, North Yorks YO12 6LA.

Springs Dance Company, Flat 2, 19 Bromley Common, Bromley BR2 9LS. (Summer school, workshops, seminars. Need to book early.)

'Body and Soul' still meets at St James' Methodist Church, High Street, Pensnett, West Midlands, every Wednesday evening at 7.30 pm. (Further details from Mrs Val Whiley.)

Andy Au, Movement in Worship, 84–86 London Road, Brighton BN1 4JF.

'Praise Him in the Dance' workshops, Christian Music Ministries, 325 Bromford Road, Hodge Hill, Birmingham B36 8ET.

Shirley Collins, 'Christian Choreographics', 'Morning Star', 9 Grange Court, Stratton, Cirencester, Glos. GL7 2JS.

Marie Bensley, Flags and Banners Focus Network Co-ordinator, Sunset Gate, St Audries, Taunton, Somerset TA4 4EA.

Regular Christian dance seminars and weekends are held at: Longmead, Milborne St Andrew, Blandford Forum, Dorset DT11 0HU.

Acknowledgements for Songs

From A Distance Words and Music by Julie Gold
Copyright © 1990 Irving Music Inc / Wing & Wheel Music / Julie Gold
Music, 50% Rondor Music (London) Ltd, SW8 4TW
Reproduced by permission of IMP Ltd.

Love Changes Everything from 'Aspects of Love'
Music: Andrew Lloyd Webber. Lyrics: Don Black and Charles Hart
Copyright © 1988. The Really Useful Group Ltd. London.
All Rights Reserved. International Copyright Secured.

Come On And Celebrate Dave Bankhead, Trish Morgan
Copyright © 1984. Kingsway's Thankyou Music, PO Box 75, Eastbourne,
East Sussex BN23 6NW, UK. Used by permission.

Lord, The Light Of Your Love Is Shining Graham Kendrick.
Copyright © 1987 Make Way Music, PO Box 263, Croydon, Surrey, CR9
5AP, UK. International copyright secured. All rights reserved.
Used by permission.

Light Of The World by D & I Butterfield
Copyright © 1980 Bible Society.

We Being Many Marty Goetz.
Copyright © 1995 Singin' in the Reign Music/Music Services. Administered
by Copycare, PO Box 77, Hailsham BN27 3EF, UK.
Used by permission.

God Is Good Graham Kendrick.
Copyright © 1985. Kingsway's Thankyou Music, PO Box 75, Eastbourne,
East Sussex BN23 6NW, UK. Used by permission.

Hosanna! John Harding
Copyright © 1975 Kingsway's Thankyou Music, PO Box 75, Eastbourne,
East Sussex BN23 6NW, UK. Used by permission.

All Heaven Declares Noel Richards, Tricia Richards
Copyright © 1987 Kingsway's Thankyou Music, PO Box 75, Eastbourne,
East Sussex BN23 6NW. Used by permission.

Peace Like A River Dave Markee, Chris Roe.
Copyright © 1990 Kingsway's Thankyou Music, PO Box 75, Eastbourne,
East Sussex BN23 6NW, UK. Used by permission.

Every effort has been made to obtain permission for all other material used.